SOME MAY ASK

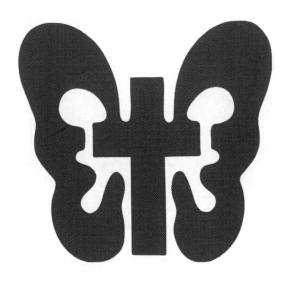

Grace Weismann

Inspiring Voices®
A Service of **Guideposts**

Inspiring Voices books may be ordered through booksellers or by contacting:

Inspiring Voices
1663 Liberty Drive
Bloomington, IN 47403
www.inspiringvoices.com
1-(866) 697-5313

Because of the dynamic nature of the Internet, any web addresses or
links contained in this book may have changed since publication and
may no longer be valid. The views expressed in this work are solely those
of the author and do not necessarily reflect the views of the publisher,
and the publisher hereby disclaims any responsibility for them.

Any people depicted in stock imagery provided by Thinkstock are
models, and such images are being used for illustrative purposes only.

Certain stock imagery © Thinkstock.

ISBN: 978-1-4624-0453-7 (e)
ISBN: 978-1-4624-0454-4 (sc)

Library of Congress Control Number: 2012922829

Printed in the United States of America

Inspiring Voices rev. date: 12/20/2012

This book is dedicated to my precious granddaughter.

*Someday you will be old enough to read this
story on your own, and you will discover
the depth of love that surrounds you.*

From the Author

Some May Ask is an answer to my prayers—in many ways. Throughout my life, I've dreamed of writing a book, and I believed I would know when there was a book to be written. As we were living the story of Emma, it became clear to me that this was a journey I needed to share. It is an inspirational story that is close to my heart, and it is a story of God's goodness. There is no doubt in my mind that this is the book I was meant to write.

Having said this, I need to acknowledge that I did not write this story alone. As each thought came to mind and as each word was written, I was mindful of the presence of the Holy Spirit. From start to finish, we worked as a team. I will be eternally grateful for this spiritual experience.

As I share this story, it is important to me to respect the privacy of those involved. Therefore, all names and some specific elements have been altered.

I thank my husband, whom I dearly love, for supporting me every step of the way—in my writing and in my life.

In addition, I thank the family members and friends who read the manuscript in its original form and offered pieces of wisdom. You know who you are. I love you all.

Finally, I praise my beloved daughter for the courage and strength she showed in the toughest of times. No one knows better than I that this was not an easy journey.

INTRODUCTION

Come into my heart and journey with me as I share the story of Emma. It is an amazing tale of faith, hope, and love interwoven into the lives of two families and one very special child. This story is a touching illustration of the miraculous work of God, the great choreographer.

I am GG, which stands for Grandma Grace. It's a name I dearly treasure because it was given to me by a family whom I have grown to love as my own. Besides being mother to four beautiful daughters, I am GG to Emma and the parents God chose for her.

If anyone had told me that my dream of being a grandmother would have followed this path, I'm not sure I would have believed it. It is not a path I would have chosen on my own, to be sure, for it was not always an easy path. Yet it was a journey that was unimaginably rich, for God was present every step of the way. There were many blessings on this path, and the gift at the end of the journey was priceless.

This is my story …

Chapter 1

It was a beautiful day in early July, the kind of summer day that makes you feel blessed and glad to be alive. Having been diagnosed the previous year with chronic lymphocytic leukemia, I was nearing the end of a six-month regimen of chemotherapy. It had been a surreal phase in my life, sort of like a timeout from the usual day-to-day existence. I was eagerly looking forward to completing my treatments, and I was praying that they had been successful. I do a lot of that—praying, I mean. My faith is at the very core of my existence. I believe in a God of great goodness ... a God of endless possibilities ... a God of hope.

On this particular summer day, I had concerns on my mind besides my health; they were *mother concerns*. My daughter Camille had moved back home months earlier to get her life back on track. Too much partying, bad relationships, and poor choices in her teen years had left her without focus, and she was ready to turn things around. Now in her early twenties, she knew that she wanted a more stable future.

In the beginning, Camille's time at home had gone well. True to her initial goals, and our parental expectations, she gave up the party life and the friends who went along with it. She seemed content to settle into the humdrum pace of our family life. She began working at a promising job that offered her a future and introduced her to young people with healthier lifestyles. After years of teenage tension, it finally seemed as if my husband, Paul, and I were beginning to develop a more open and honest relationship with our daughter. We were proud of her efforts to become a responsible adult.

More recently, however, there had been a change in Camille. She had become moody and difficult to get along with. She continued to go to work faithfully each day but spent most of her time at home in her room, coming out only to grab a bite to eat. The destructive behaviors had not returned, yet her troubled spirit worried me. Paul and I were concerned, but any attempts to connect with Camille on an emotional level proved unsuccessful. I kept asking myself, "What is wrong?" And I prayed.

I don't remember what I was doing at the exact moment the answer came to me. It's not unusual for me to be alerted by a significant thought in an otherwise insignificant moment. It's as if I become aware of a gentle voice calling to me. More than spoken words, it's a feeling that says, "Pay attention—this is important!" I have learned to do just that. Nevertheless, I was stunned with disbelief as the thought came to me out of the blue: "Camille is pregnant". Call me naive, but the possibility of pregnancy had never even occurred to me. Because of this, I rejected the idea at first, refusing to believe it could be true.

How could it be? Camille hadn't dated in more than eight months. She had a small build and showed no physical signs of being pregnant. It just didn't seem possible to me. In the days ahead, however, I began to notice some things that made me wonder. Camille had been complaining of a sore hip and walked with a different gait. She wore only loose clothing. Although it was nothing remarkable, she had put on a little weight. She continued to work her early morning shift, but she slept much of the rest of the day; it seemed as if she was always tired. And the moodiness … recently it seemed as if the moodiness had a new dimension to it. Could it be fear?

I wanted to put these concerns out of my mind, but the voice was persistent. After struggling with the possibility of pregnancy, and considering the ramifications if it were true, I knew I had to talk with Camille. I went to her room and surprised us both by asking, "Are you pregnant?" Her response was even more surprising: "How did you know?" I honestly didn't know how to answer.

The days ahead were like a dream. I kept hoping I would wake up at any moment and breathe a sigh of relief. But that didn't happen, of course. This was real life. Once the shock wore off, Paul and I sat down together to rationally discuss the situation. We shared a commitment to support Camille on this unexpected journey, and we agreed that our response needed to be positive and genuine. We wanted to create a healthy support system for Camille, as well as for the precious life that was growing inside the womb of our very frightened daughter.

SOME MAY ASK ...

> "How is it possible that you didn't know Camille was pregnant?"

TO YOU I SAY ...

> "That's a question I have asked myself time and time again."

CHAPTER 2

If you believe, as I do, that blessings come from each difficult situation in life, you will understand my reason for telling this story. If you share my respect for the faithfulness of God, you will be in awe of his works—though not at all surprised at what he can do to bring goodness into life's challenges. I directly experienced God's amazing handiwork on this journey, as he worked miracles—both large and small—in the lives of those I love.

Let me share a little about my Camille. Throughout the years, I have told Camille that there is a special pocket of love in my heart just for her. Camille came into our family when she was just five months old. Born far away, she was placed for adoption by two young parents who, unmarried and unable to raise a child on their own, wanted her to have all she deserved in life. That's where we came in. We were a family of four—a caring couple blessed with two young, "homegrown" daughters—who had a lot more love to share. We wanted to share that love with a child who needed us.

Camille's beginning months in life had not been easy. She had spent the first weeks with her paternal grandparents, who had tried their best to care for her but were unable to make it work at their late stage in life. She was then placed in an orphanage before being assigned to a temporary foster family who, we were told, adored her. When we were selected as a good match for her, Camille was taken back to the orphanage in preparation for her journey home to us, her forever family. That's a great deal of upheaval for an infant, especially during the developmental period in life when trust is formed through stable relationships.

As a mother, I was already aware of the importance of loving and secure relationships in an infant's early months. However, in my efforts to learn all I could about adoption, I discovered that the absence of strong, connecting relationships in the early months can lead to emotional issues as a child develops. Essentially, our ability to emotionally attach to others throughout our lives depends on those early attachments. This is an important piece of knowledge for adoptive parents.

In the many months that we waited for our dream to be fulfilled, I prayed often for our child-to-be, her birth family, and those who were caring for her before she came to us. Those prayers kept her present to me at all times. "God," I pleaded, "please make sure our little girl is getting all she deserves during this time. Please see that her physical and emotional needs are being met each and every moment."

~ 🦋 ~

I will never forget the day our tiny Camille arrived on that huge airplane, along with many other children coming to join their new families. We were so excited to greet our little sweetheart with hugs and kisses! Each of us was eager to shower her with love. She was our daughter—and Beth's and Rebecca's sister—just as surely as if we were bringing her home from the hospital. We had spent months preparing for this moment, in our home and in our hearts, and we were thrilled that this day had finally arrived.

Camille, however, was in a different emotional space. While we were creating a place for her, she was enduring more dramatic changes in her brief life than most experience in a lifetime. I will always remember the look on her face as we knelt over her for the first time. Her confused little eyes seemed to say, "Who are you and how do you fit into my world?"

From that initial moment of wonder, through the weeks and months that followed, Camille became acquainted with a large network of people who would grow to love her. There were grandparents, aunts, uncles, and cousins eager to welcome her into the family. There were close friends waiting to see the little one who had been in their prayers. It was a joyful time in our lives. God had truly blessed us all.

As time passed, the young child who had come to us stiff and confused soon began to relax and grow more comfortable with each new day. Yet the influence of those first uncertain months of life would be with Camille for many years to come.

SOME MAY ASK ...

> "Did you ever fear that you could not love your
> adopted child as much as you loved her sisters?"

TO YOU I SAY ...

> "Whatever fears I may have had instantly melted
> away the moment I first held Camille in my arms
> and looked into her eyes. My love for her—and
> each of her sisters—continues to grow with each
> passing day."

CHAPTER 3

From the moment we learned that Camille was pregnant, our lives changed forever. None of us could have imagined what would lie ahead. During one of our initial conversations about the pregnancy, Camille told me she thought the baby was due soon. She shared that she had been in a brief relationship with the father more than eight months earlier and had not been with him, or anyone else, since. Camille also said she was certain the baby's father would not welcome the news that he had a child on the way.

While Paul and I were concerned that she had kept the secret to herself for so long and had received no prenatal care, we were thankful Camille had chosen to carry the baby. When I assured her that she was no longer alone, I could see Camille's immense relief. It seemed as if, right before my eyes, she began to shed the stiff protective shell she had worn in recent months. This was a shell that I had become accustomed to over the years. In times of fear and uncertainty, Camille tended to pull away emotionally and reach for that shell; it was a coping mechanism that had most likely been planted in those early months of her life. Now, as I saw her start to relax, my heart ached to think of the many lonely and frightened months Camille had spent without the support she needed. This was no time for regret, however. We needed to be positive and strong. And we needed to put our faith in God.

From the beginning of this journey, I had a sense of a bigger picture. It wasn't just about an unplanned pregnancy and the stress of everything that needed to be done. It seemed clear to me that God was busy at work. I truly felt as if we were being guided on this new path, a path that would eventually involve the lives of many. I never questioned why; on some level, I knew. There was a purpose here, and God would be our source of strength and direction.

And so it was that, hand in hand, we took those first steps. Because Camille had not received the essential prenatal care that she and her baby needed, a visit to the doctor was first on the agenda. Whatever choice she made about the future, it was important to make sure that she and the baby were healthy. We were blessed to find a wonderful OB/ GYN office in our part of town. I'm not sure what I had been expecting, but I was pleasantly surprised. From that first appointment, Camille was treated with an abundance of respect and support from the medical community. Where she had feared judgment and disapproval, she was met with professionalism and compassion. I was extremely grateful for the tender spirit of each and every person who helped my daughter.

After her initial appointment, Camille came to me and shared that she had made her decision about the baby. She sobbed as she told me she was not prepared to raise a child. She knew she couldn't give her baby everything it needed and deserved. By her own admission, Camille still felt like a kid herself, struggling to grow up. She wanted this baby to have a mother and father who were ready and willing to be good parents. With tears in her eyes, she told me, "Adoption is the only answer." When I asked Camille if she wanted to look into an open adoption, which would allow her to be part of her baby's life, she told me that she would not even consider it. I could tell the concept seemed much too painful for her.

Camille was beginning to comprehend the intensity of the situation that her own birth parents had faced. Perhaps for the first time, she understood what a difficult and unselfish decision they had made. Camille wanted her baby to have the opportunities she had been given in life. She wanted the child to know the love and security she had known. I saw the pain in her eyes, and I knew this was not an easy thing for her to do. And yet, deep in my heart, I knew it was the best decision she could make.

Although Camille would tell you she does not have a strong faith, I believe that during those difficult moments of indecision she had received guidance from a God who continually watches over her. I knew God was now watching over her child, as well. Paul and I were relieved about Camille's decision, and we were thankful for the help she had received in making it. This mature decision was the first of many that would follow as the journey continued.

SOME MAY ASK ...

> *"Did you ever consider raising the baby yourself?"*

TO YOU I SAY ...

> *"Yes—for a brief, heart-wrenching moment."*

CHAPTER 4

As much as I yearned to be a grandmother (and believe me, I was *yearning*), I quickly reminded myself that this was not about my desire for a grandchild. After the initial consideration of possibilities and much discussion, Paul and I knew that raising the baby ourselves was not an option we could present to Camille. As I completed chemotherapy and awaited test results to see if my cancer was in remission, my future was uncertain.

It was more than that, though. Paul and I had always been in agreement that our children should raise their children. Each of us looked forward to being a grandparent more than I can say. However, as we saw the complications that arose when friends stepped into the parenting role with their grandchildren, we told our girls that we would not take on that responsibility. I can understand why it may seem necessary to take that path in certain circumstances, and I don't sit in judgment of those who have made that choice. But it did not feel right for us.

Once Camille had made her decision, there were many more challenges to face. She knew what she wanted for her baby, but we needed to find out where to go for help. Calls were made to adoption agencies and questions were asked. We learned a lot about the process, but nothing "clicked." By this I mean that we were doing the groundwork, but I knew the real work would come from God. He would let us know when we were on the correct path. So the prayers continued: for a healthy baby, for guidance and direction, and now for the parents who would be blessed with this child.

It didn't take long for the prayers for direction to be answered. Camille unlocked that door herself. She would tell you that the answer just came to her and she doesn't know why. I have my own thoughts about the matter. During this journey, I saw Camille as a precious vessel—in spirit, as well as in body. Unknowingly, she was allowing God to work through her. It was not a conscious decision on her part.

And so it was that Camille suggested we call a dear family friend whom she knew I trusted very much. Although she had not seen Nathan since she was a young child, he came to her mind. A respected lawyer and a deacon in his church, Nathan was a wise and compassionate man. Paul and I thought the world of him, and Camille knew that. "Maybe Nathan can tell us what to do," she said. Once she made the suggestion, which sounded perfect to me, we were on the phone to Nathan. Across the miles, Camille explained her situation.

Always sensitive to others, Nathan listened carefully as Camille told him she was looking for a couple to adopt the baby she was carrying. He didn't seem shocked, as she had secretly feared. Rather, he told Camille that he had a story to share with her. Nathan revealed to Camille that she had played a significant role in his life. He and his wife, Julia, who was also a dear friend, were among those who had been praying for Camille while we waited for her to join us. Nathan explained that when he and Julia saw how much joy Camille brought to our family, they made a decision to adopt a child of their own. Their Molly had come to them as a newborn and was just a few years younger than Camille.

Camille had not been aware of this. I'm not sure that her dad and I were even aware of this, but hearing those words brought my attention, once again, to God's choreography in this dance of life. It was one of those moments—and there would be many in the months ahead—where the mind sighs *ahhh* and the heart hums. It is an inward experience of God's presence.

To say that Nathan was a tremendous help would be a huge understatement. He soon became an integral part of the plan that was now in play. A man of faith, Nathan asked Camille to give him some time for prayer and contemplation. As we waited, Camille and I settled into a place of peace. I suspect that Camille's peace came from knowing the situation was in good hands with Nathan. For me, it was a matter of patiently waiting for God to do his work. This was one of those periods when I was showered with a familiar sense of awe and wonder. I waited, knowing that everything was going to work out the way it was meant to be. It was like waiting for a miracle that you knew was going to happen.

SOME MAY ASK ...

> *"Were you nervous about finding the right parents for the baby?"*

TO YOU I SAY ...

> *"Never. From the very beginning, I trusted in God's plan for this child."*

CHAPTER 5

In the meantime, I counted our blessings. Camille had made a wise decision about her baby and had found a reliable resource in Nathan. Additionally, we had learned at Camille's first doctor's appointment that both she and the baby were in good health. I felt a huge sense of relief upon hearing this; I was well aware that it could have been a completely different scenario. Time and time again, I was overcome with an abundance of gratitude.

Looking at her tummy, I wondered how Camille could possibly be in the last month of pregnancy, as she suspected. To my amazement, however, tests confirmed that the baby was almost full term; Camille would most likely deliver within the month. I was instantly overwhelmed. A great deal needed to happen within that month to prepare for this baby. I'm not talking about the normal set-up-the-nursery kinds of things. We needed to make sure the baby's adoptive parents were waiting with open arms. "God," I prayed, "we don't have much time!" As if I needed to tell him …

I want to take a moment here to emphasize that I am sharing this story from *my* perspective, through the eyes of my faith. But I don't want to minimize the fact that this was not an easy time for Camille. While we experienced a special closeness as mother and daughter—which was a blessing to each of us—her personal journey was deeply emotional, as well as physical. I understood completely, and my heart often ached for her.

Struggling to distance herself from the baby she was carrying, Camille didn't want to know if it was a boy or a girl. She told me that she didn't want to see the baby or hold it after it was born. It was clear to me that she needed to keep the baby separate from herself in order to soften the inevitable heartache that would come later. I suggested that it would be a good idea for her to talk with a professional to help her work through the difficult issues she was facing, but she rejected the idea. Camille was going to deal with this in her own way, just as she had always dealt with the challenges in her life. I could offer motherly suggestions, but the choices were ultimately hers to make.

I was feeling especially sad the day Camille had the ultrasound that would give her a more specific due date. How I wished the situation was different, that Camille had a loving husband at her side and together they were joyfully anticipating the birth of their child. Instead, I gently held her hand as she sobbed throughout the procedure. I think it began to sink in at this point: there was a little life inside her that would soon be making its entrance into the world. This was not how either of us had imagined things would be. My daughter was carrying a child that neither of us would ever know. I shared her pain.

Just as Camille had suspected, the ultrasound revealed that her baby's due date was not far off. She had two—possibly three—weeks before she would deliver. Once again, I felt an immediate sense of panic; there wasn't going to be much time for us to put things in order. Then I reminded myself that God was at the helm. He knew what needed to happen, even if we did not. I was thankful to be able to place it all in his hands. My personal challenge, however, was to *completely* let it go.

After eight months of keeping this secret to herself, Camille was thankful for our support. She still didn't want others to know that she was pregnant, however. She told only her work manager, who had been very understanding when Camille asked for a month off. Although we were conflicted, Paul and I honored her request for secrecy. Even her youngest sister Sadie, who had joined the family later in Camille's life and still lived at home, was kept in the dark. I didn't like the idea of a family secret; it went against everything I believed in. But Paul and I agreed that we needed to respect Camille's request.

SOME MAY ASK ...

> *"Was it difficult to honor Camille's wishes when they differed from your own?"*

TO YOU I SAY ...

> *"Yes, it was. But I knew that the decisions were hers to make."*

CHAPTER 6

It was not long after Camille had spoken to Nathan that he called to tell us about a prospective adoptive couple who belonged to his church. Nathan had learned about their situation from his pastor, who knew that this couple's dream of starting a family had eluded them for many years. Ben and Rachel were in their late thirties and had been married for almost ten years. "Rachel teaches young children in a Christian school. Ben has just started a new business, in addition to working in construction. They're both active in our church, and Ben also coaches youth sports," Nathan told Camille. He went on to say that Ben's parents live in another part of the country, but Rachel's retired parents live near them and operate a daycare for young children in their home.

Nathan shared that Ben and Rachel had been trying to start a family for most of their married life but had not been successful. Rachel had suffered through multiple miscarriages and had recently been told by her doctor that the pregnancies were taking a toll on her body. He strongly advised her to avoid getting pregnant again. This had been devastating news to the couple, who yearned desperately for a baby of their own. At this point in time, they were grieving for what was never to be and wondering how they would ever overcome the emptiness they were feeling in their hearts.

As Camille told me about her conversation with Nathan, a smile came to my lips and I was filled with hope. Could this be the couple God had chosen for her baby? In my mind, I saw an image of God—all-knowing and all-powerful—watching from above. The ultimate source of love, our God saw a young woman with a precious gift to give and a young couple so very ready to receive. In his wisdom, he knew that all would be well. In my faith, I knew he could make it so.

Although Camille didn't need much time to make her decision, she did take a day to think everything through. She wanted to be thorough, to make sure she was doing the right thing for her baby. I was very proud of her. Camille did not take the situation lightly; she understood the impact of her decision on each of the lives involved. After considerable thought, she called Nathan to tell him that she would like Ben and Rachel to be her baby's parents. It was such a simple statement with such incredible possibilities.

The wheels quickly began to turn following that phone call to Nathan. After talking with Camille, he made the memorable call to Ben and Rachel, who had no idea they were being considered as parents for Camille's baby. Over the phone, Nathan told them that a baby would soon be born, and the birth mother would like them to be its parents. *Can you imagine*? I often sit back and wonder what that call must have been like for them. In the depth of their grief, when their dream of a baby seemed hopeless, they receive a phone call with the most miraculous news. There was a child waiting to be born into their lives! It is all so amazing to me.

It was not a surprise when Nathan phoned with the news that Ben and Rachel were ecstatic. Yes! They wanted, more than anything else in the world, to welcome Camille's child into their hearts and their home. They were so grateful for this miracle!

With their lives taking a remarkable new turn, Ben and Rachel immediately began the process of a home study that would assure Camille that a good choice had been made. Calls announcing the pending birth were made to their family and friends, who were in awe at the joyful news. Recently burdened with sadness and despair, this couple was now overflowing with a spirit of joy and celebration! And so it was that many more prayers—prayers of thanksgiving and praise—were sent to the God of goodness and grace.

In addition to offering those prayers, family and friends rallied around this young couple they loved so much. They came to their home to share hugs of congratulations and to offer support. There was laughter and joy and love—*lots of love*! Ben and Rachel, bathed in that love, began to imagine their home and their lives blessed with a child. A miracle was unfolding. There was much to be done to prepare for the child that God was bringing to them. But there would be time—or so they thought.

SOME MAY ASK ...

> *"Did you ever have any doubts that these were the right parents for Camille's baby?"*

TO YOU I SAY ...

> *"Not once. That is the beauty of turning things over to a wise and faithful God."*

CHAPTER 7

While a home far away was bubbling with anticipation and happiness, I was doing my best to support Camille. I wanted to make sure she was rested and comfortable in the short time before the baby was to arrive. I bought her some cute maternity tops and was surprised to see her quickly begin to fill them out. With the decision about the baby's parents in place, there was another wave of peace. This was a pleasant time.

Nathan had told Camille that she would need to see an attorney to get things in place for the adoption. He gave her the name of a well-respected lawyer with whom he had previously shared an office. Once again, we felt blessed to be connected with professional and compassionate people. I thanked God for his ongoing guidance. He was working through all the people he placed in our path, and I knew this. I was well aware that occurrences seen by some as coincidence were actually the work of God, whom I trusted with all my heart. I would rely on this trust even more heavily in the future as new challenges arose.

It was in our meeting with Christine, the attorney Nathan had recommended, that we learned what we should have considered all along. Because she had decided upon adoption for her baby, Camille was required by law to divulge the name of David, the baby's father. It was his right to be informed of the pending birth and to have a voice in the situation. Of course, it made sense. Camille, however, had extremely negative feelings about the baby's father, and she wanted nothing to do with him. Because of this, it was decided that Christine would contact David and apprise him of the situation. Shaken by these new circumstances, all we could do was hope that he would consent to the baby's adoption.

As I travel through a life with challenges, I always try to put myself in the position of others and see things from their point of view. I could not, however, even begin to comprehend how a young man would feel upon receiving this message from a stranger: "You have fathered a child that is about to be born." I have no doubt that Christine was very sensitive when speaking to David. However, there was no time to let him digest that news before telling him that Camille wanted to place the baby for adoption. I am certain this was more than he could handle.

Understandably, this is where our journey took a turn from unexpected blessings to extreme challenge. The situation was not going to be as smooth as I had hoped, but I knew from past experience that God does not always arrange for smooth sailing. He, alone, knows the reasoning behind the events that must play out in the big picture. To be honest, I don't welcome the rocky roads in life, but I try not to question God's intentions. I trust him completely, and on this day I vowed to put my faith in his wisdom once again.

As Camille's due date drew near, I knew that David was trying to wrap his mind around the news he had recently been given. Christine told Camille that he had refused to even consider allowing his baby to be adopted. Understandably, he was angry with Camille for not telling him about the baby earlier and for refusing to speak with him now. Yet he expressed to Christine that he cared deeply for Camille and was confident this baby would bring her back into his life.

David continued to try to make contact with Camille, and she continued to avoid him. There was more to their brief relationship than I knew—I understood that—but her rejection only seemed to make matters worse. I often wonder if things might have been easier if Camille had just made the effort to communicate with David. As it was, he came to the erroneous conclusion that Camille had been purposefully deceitful, that she had made adoption plans with Ben and Rachel early on in the pregnancy. It seemed rather convoluted, but then I imagine the shock of the situation didn't lend itself to clear thinking.

With Camille's permission, I met with David. I was convinced that if I reached out to him in a warm and sincere manner, we could shift the negative direction the situation was taking. Our visit began with cordial small talk that seemed comfortable for both of us, and then David talked a bit about his family. Although he didn't go into specifics, it was clear that there had been many challenges in his life. Eventually, the conversation turned to Camille and the baby. I gently explained to David that no one except Camille knew about this baby until recently. I assured him that I understood why he was angry to learn about the situation from an attorney and not from Camille herself. We went on to discuss the issue of adoption—at great length. The visit ended amicably. Prior to our conversation, I had truly believed that if David was encouraged to consider what was best for this baby, he would agree to the adoption. I was wrong.

SOME MAY ASK …

> "Did you tell the parents-in-waiting about this new development?"

TO YOU I SAY …

> "Not at this point. I prayed with all my might that David would change his mind."

CHAPTER 8

Time was passing quickly. It had been less than two weeks since Paul and I first learned that a baby was on the way, and a lot had happened in that short period. It was now becoming clear to me that what I saw as God's plan for this baby was going to be complicated. The new development with David, however, did not cause me to lose faith in what I strongly felt was meant to be. All we could do at this point was go with the flow—and trust.

It had been less than one week since Ben and Rachel had learned about the baby. I continued to imagine their joyful anticipation, and I prayed that God would make his presence known to all of us as his plan unfolded. Camille didn't seem to have a feeling of connection to her child at this point; she said that she was just eager to have the experience over. My heart was hurting a lot now—for my child and for the grandchild I would never know. I tried to focus on the task at hand, which was to support my daughter, but I could not deny the strong feelings that were churning inside me.

On one particular day, I was struggling to get back on my feet following a chemotherapy treatment. Although it normally took a week to get my strength back, I knew that this treatment cycle had to be different. I didn't have a full week to get strong, nor would I be able to stay isolated for the second week, as recommended because of my compromised immune system. Just as God was watching over Camille and her baby, however, I knew he was going to watch over me and protect me when I needed it.

Sensing that protection, which truly feels as if his arms are around me, I told Camille that it would be a good idea for us to go to the library and check out a video on childbirth. I wanted her to have some idea of what was going to happen when the baby was born so she would feel more confident during the process. I still smile when I think of her response. It was so like Camille to say, "Thanks, Mom, but I just want to do this *cold turkey.*" Although I chuckled, I was adamant when I explained to her that giving birth was not something you went into without some kind of preparation. Perhaps it was the teacher in me, but I wanted Camille to have as much information as possible when it was time for her baby to arrive.

We headed to the library, and I was relieved when I saw the childbirth video on the shelf. Once back home, we sat together on the bed and began watching. It was a tender time for me. Although it was outdated, the video brought back memories of the births of Camille's two older sisters. Childbirth is such a sacred experience. I prayed at the time that Camille would be able to have a sense of that sacredness when the time came for her to give birth. As we continued, however, I could see that for Camille this was merely a "how to" video, an educational film. We watched for what seemed like a very long time before we decided to take a break and finish watching the next day.

I was glad that we had seen as much of the video as we had because it gave Camille some valuable information, but we never had the opportunity to see the remainder of the film. Following an afternoon nap, Camille complained of stomach pains that felt to her like intense gas bubbles. When the pains had not gone away by early evening, we called the hospital. We were told that it was probably just false labor since Camille had not yet reached full term in her pregnancy.

The pains intensified, however, and at midnight we headed to the hospital. Upon her arrival, Camille was immediately admitted and taken to the maternity floor. We were stunned. I remember telling the nurses that we weren't ready for this baby. I told them there was going to be an adoption and things were not yet in place. They assured me that everything was going to be okay and focused on taking care of my frightened daughter.

Unknown to any of us, Camille was beginning an experience that would bring her full circle in her young life. I let go of my panic, surrendering my concern for the baby, Camille, David, and the adoptive parents. I knew God was watching over us all.

Some may ask …

"*What were you feeling as the birthing process began?*"

To you I say …

"*It all seemed like a dream to me. I remember a sense of numbness as the situation unfolded on its own. Somewhere deep inside, I was filled with great anticipation. I realized I was very eager to meet this child!*"

CHAPTER 9

The hours that followed were surreal. Camille was drawn into a physical experience for which she was not totally prepared, despite genuine efforts to lay the groundwork. Yet she managed to come through it with strength and courage. She was treated compassionately by everyone involved—especially her new doctor, who came to the hospital on his day off to deliver her baby. Camille was blessed with an abundance of encouragement and respect. I could tell this left a deep impression on her.

The labor continued on for more than twelve hours. As the contractions intensified, I could see that Camille was beginning to wonder if her baby would ever arrive. Although I was at her side during the labor, I had expected to be out in the hall with Paul when the baby was born. When Camille asked me to stay with her during the delivery, I was deeply touched. I could see in her eyes that she was apprehensive. I was honored to be able to hold her hand and comfort her during the actual birth of her daughter.

Yes, Camille's baby was a beautiful little girl. After many hours of waiting, and following those intense final moments of delivery, an angel was born. I say that with sincerity because this infant, whom Camille initially never intended to see or hold, would do the work of an angel on earth in a very short time. She would soften a hardened heart and bring healing to a troubled soul. Without even being aware of the effect her child would have on her, Camille actually began calling this precious child "my little angel." That would be her only name until she left Camille's arms.

As any parent or grandparent will tell you, childbirth is a miraculous experience. Beyond the anticipated miracle of this birth, however, a deeper miracle evolved. Camille had entered the hospital with her protective shell. As I mentioned earlier, she wore it close to her when she was afraid and uncertain. I often felt helpless at these times and could only be patient and loving until Camille was ready to let her guard down. On this day in Camille's young life, however, a tiny baby girl broke through that armor. I could not have imagined, in my wildest dreams, the power this child would have.

After her baby was born, an exhausted Camille looked at me and asked, "Mom, would you like to be the first to hold her?" I must admit that I was walking an uncertain path up to this point, taking my cues from Camille. I had understood earlier why she had said she didn't want a connection with her baby; I knew it was to ease the pain of losing her. Yet now I was sensing a change in my daughter. Camille was clearly asking me to cross the line that she had previously drawn. With a silent prayer of thanksgiving, I took Camille's baby in my arms and looked into her beautiful face. Tears fell.

It's difficult to describe the multitude of feelings I experienced while holding Camille's daughter. I can only say that I was in complete awe. I knew this was a very significant moment, one that I would cherish over and over again in years to come. I wanted Paul to share in this joy, so I was glad when Camille suggested that he hold her baby. As the tiny infant went from my arms to his, Camille and I watched him struggle with emotion. Through his tears, Paul softly told his granddaughter, "Welcome to the world, little one."

When it was time for the newborn's first bath and feeding, Camille encouraged Paul to carry her baby to the nursery. After the nurses bathed her, he fed her and rocked her as she slept. In the meantime, I sat beside Camille and stroked her hand as she fell in and out of much-needed sleep. These quiet moments gave me time to try to comprehend what had just taken place in my little world. A nine-month pregnancy before birth is filled with anticipation and preparation, emotional and otherwise. My own two weeks with Camille's pregnancy had been a whirlwind. As I looked down at my sleeping daughter, I wondered what things felt like in her world.

SOME MAY ASK …

> "Were you surprised at Paul's reaction to all that
> was happening?"

TO YOU I SAY …

> "Paul is a rational man; he is my 'rock' and the
> foundation of strength and wisdom in our family.
> I underestimated the effect this experience would
> have on him. As his granddaughter was born
> and he held her close, he was overwhelmed with
> emotion and love for this new little life. His
> reaction deeply touched my heart."

CHAPTER 10

When she was fully awake, Camille told me she wanted to hold her baby. I was a bit surprised, yet I think I had expected her to have this change of heart. Perhaps I had secretly hoped for it, knowing that it was an important piece of Camille's emotional healing surrounding the adoption of her baby. Whatever the reason, I knew that it would be a blessing for each of them to experience the tender touch between mother and child.

I walked into the nursery where Paul had been rocking the sweet little bundle for quite a while. Touched by the sight of the two of them, I stood there quietly and watched. I could see that my husband's heart was fully engaged as he gazed down at the tiny infant, and I secretly ached for him. He had been swept up in this rush of emotion, just as Camille and I had, and he would also be feeling great loss in the days ahead.

Paul looked up at me and smiled his beautiful smile. When I told him that Camille wanted to hold her baby, I detected a sense of relief. We both felt it. We wanted this experience to be positive for Camille, as well as her baby. Together we took Camille's newborn daughter to her waiting arms, and we watched for a moment as she held her baby close. Soon we left the room to give the two of them special time alone. Something wonderful must have happened during those moments they were alone together, because we returned later to find the baby's bassinet stationed in the room. Camille wanted to be near her baby. I had no doubt that God was responsible.

Many phone calls were made that afternoon. Rebecca and Sadie, two of Camille's sisters, and one of her dearest friends were called to the hospital "to meet someone special." As unbelievable as it sounds, none of these young women were aware that Camille had been pregnant. I had no idea how these unveiling moments were going to play out, and I prayed there would be acceptance and love in that hospital room when they arrived. My prayers were answered. There was amazement and disbelief ("How did we not know?" "*Why* did we not know?") and there were many tears of joy surrounding the miracle of this new life. Thankfully, there was also immediate love for this new little niece who was not destined to be in their lives.

Each visit seemed to bring a gentle explosion of emotion, and God's handiwork was quite evident. I've always loved the analogy of the tapestry of life. Perhaps you've heard it. It compares each individual life to a tapestry: we see the underside of our creation, with tangled threads and knots and imperfection, but God sees only the topside, the

beautifully finished product. This is how I would describe our afternoon in the hospital. If ever there was the potential to see tangled threads and knots and imperfection in people, it was then. But we only experienced goodness—God's goodness.

Lest I portray a situation that was all sweet and rosy, let me share that a call made later in the afternoon did not go as well. Many miles away, Camille's oldest sister was shocked to receive this news over the phone. Beth had always been a loving "second mother" to her adopted sister. From the moment Camille joined our family, Beth had taken her under her wing. They shared a very special connection. To hear that Camille had given birth to a baby, with no knowledge that she had been pregnant, was difficult for Beth. In addition, the miles between us did not allow her to come to the hospital to see the baby and hold her in her arms. Beth experienced the shock of the unexpected birth but was not able to experience the sense of miracle that came with it. I understood why she was hurt.

The most significant phone call Camille made that afternoon was to Christine, her attorney, who was asked to share the good news with the adoptive couple. Imagine— just one week after being told they were going to be parents, Ben and Rachel would receive the news that their healthy baby girl had arrived. What immeasurable joy that phone call would bring! As each of us in that hospital room took turns holding Camille's little one, I prayed for the new parents who would soon reach out for her. I also prayed for

~ 🦋 ~

all of us—for the strength and the courage we would need to relinquish this child, whom we already loved so dearly, into their waiting arms.

Finally, at the end of an extremely emotional day, another call needed to be made. Christine called David to tell him that the baby had been born. His response was expected. He wanted to see his daughter.

SOME MAY ASK ...

> "*Were you hoping that David wouldn't be interested in seeing his baby?*"

TO YOU I SAY ...

> "*We had no right to hope for that. All of us knew that once David met his child, however, his heart would engage as ours had. We feared that difficult times lay ahead. We were correct.*"

CHAPTER 11

During the day and a half we spent in the hospital with Camille's little angel, it seemed as if time stood still. I was thankful for that. We needed the time to absorb all that was taking place. Although none of us had expected it to happen the way it did, our family had fallen in love with this beautiful child. We knew she would always be part of us, even though we believed we would never see her again. It was important to take the time to welcome her into our lives, if only for a short time. Most important of all for the baby, Camille needed the time to bond with her little one, and I was thankful she was willing to allow that to happen.

As the hours passed, it was common—and very touching—to see Camille hold her baby close, always on the left side of her chest with the tiny infant's face toward her own. I remember thinking that it seemed like she was holding her baby close to her heart. It looked so comfortable and natural for both of them, like they had been together forever. There was a sense of peacefulness between them that is difficult to describe. It was as if—for this brief period in time—they were one, bonding in love as it was intended to be. Those moments were a gift given to both by the God who had brought them together. And those of us who were present were gifted, as well.

I have precious photographs of those hours in the hospital. I keep them in a little pink photo album with the word *LOVE* embroidered on the front. Most of the pictures show smiles and joy, but there are a few that reveal the underlying sadness. There is one picture of Camille holding her baby that somehow captures each and every one of the intense emotions she was feeling at the time: love, sadness, fear. I treasure that picture, and yet it breaks my heart to look at it.

When I look back on Camille's special time with her daughter, I am especially moved by the words she spoke to her child. As I sat quietly nearby, Camille looked into her baby's eyes and poured out her soul. She talked openly to her little one as if no one else was in the room. Speaking from a deep and vulnerable place I had rarely seen before, Camille told her baby she loved her more than she ever thought it was possible to love someone, and she wanted her to have the best in life. She wanted her to have two parents who were stable and happy and could give her what she needed. Camille told her, "I want you to have what I have. I want you to feel secure and loved."

At this moment, I realized that Camille's journey along life's often-bumpy road had brought her full circle. It was a beautiful realization to behold. All these years, especially during the tough times, I had been deeply worried that my daughter had not experienced the necessary bonding during those first few months before she came to us; it is a concern not uncommon for adoptive parents. But on this miraculous day, as I watched Camille speak lovingly to her child, I knew for certain what I had desperately needed to know.

Camille had clearly made important emotional connections with those who had cared for her in her early months. Perhaps her opportunities to bond had been sporadic or inconsistent according to normal standards, but they had made a difference. They had left a significant imprint on my child's life. On some level, Camille was now reaching into the past, into a time that had been lovingly orchestrated for her. It was here that she found what she needed to be able to bond with her child in the present.

And the cycle would continue, for Camille's baby was now receiving exactly what *she* needed to be an emotionally healthy human being. Very simply, it was love. I marveled at the revelation that was playing out before me. I marveled at God's amazing grace. Once again, my prayers for my daughter had been answered.

SOME MAY ASK …

> *"Did you ever think that Camille might decide to keep her baby?"*

TO YOU I SAY …

> *"I truly wondered if that was going to happen. After hours of holding her baby close, however, Camille tearfully repeated that she knew her baby deserved more than she was able to give her. And so, she followed through with the hardest decision she had ever had to make. Although it was extremely difficult for all of us, we knew it was for the best."*

CHAPTER 12

Although he was absent from the hospital scene, David was always in the back of my mind. Camille clearly did not want to deal with him, but I was never—even for a moment—unmindful of his place in the scenario. His relationship with Camille, though brief and uncommitted, had produced a child. David was the baby's biological father, and he had rights that needed to be honored. This was conflicting for me because I shared Camille's belief that the child deserved to be raised by two mature parents who loved their daughter *and* each other.

Please understand that I am not, by any means, against single parents raising children, but parenting is a challenge even for those who are prepared. Camille and David were both young and unsettled; they were still in the process of evolving into adults. Having worked with at-risk families in the past, I knew all too well what happens to children when their parents are not ready to take on the responsibility of parenting. Sadly, I still remember the faces and broken spirits of those children who were torn between battling parents.

The thought of this precious child growing up in the midst of turmoil and strife broke my heart. She deserved much better than that. All children do.

This was on my mind when Camille made the decision that she wanted her baby to go home from the hospital with the parents who were ready to welcome her into their lives. Because of the uncertainty of the situation with David, temporary foster care was presented to Camille as an option, but that was inconceivable to her—and to me. As you can imagine, neither of us wanted this child to go through a series of placements that would create an unsettled path to her adoption. It was a painful and all-too-familiar prospect.

Camille also had the option of bringing her baby to our home until the situation was settled. I must admit that pleasant thoughts of additional time with the sweet infant came to mind, but I wondered if our hearts could handle it. We had already developed a great deal of love for this little child. To bring her into our home and then have to let her go seemed like an impossible scenario. I couldn't even imagine how difficult that would be.

In the end, Camille was adamant about what she wanted for her baby, and I was proud of her tenacity. I knew that her intentions at this point, as all along, were centered on what was best for her child. As the birth mother, she signed the temporary paperwork needed for the baby to leave the hospital with the prospective adoptive parents. The paternity of the father had not been officially determined, and the paternity test would take approximately two weeks to complete. Because of this, Camille could legally make the decision alone.

It was now time to face the fact that Christine needed to call Ben and Rachel, who were anxiously waiting to hear what the next step would be, and give them the troubling news about David. We had put the call off, hoping he would change his mind, but we could no longer keep his intentions from them. Christine gently conveyed to them that the birth father was resisting the idea of giving up his baby, but Camille was determined to pursue the adoption. Christine told Ben and Rachel, "It's now up to the two of you to decide if you want to continue." She explained to them that if they were willing to take the risk that David would change his mind, it was Camille's desire for the baby to leave the hospital with them. There was no hesitation at all; this was their desire, as well. They desperately wanted this baby, and they would go through whatever steps it took to make her part of their family.

Out of respect for David, Christine notified him of Camille's wish for the baby to leave the hospital with Ben and Rachel. Although it was not legally necessary to get his permission, he agreed to the arrangement. Once again, he asked to see his daughter. We were thankful he was willing to wait until she was out of the hospital. It was our sincere hope that once David met Ben and Rachel with the baby and could see for himself what good and loving people they were, he would agree that adoption was in the

~ 🦋 ~

best interest of the child. We realized, however, that this
was a lot to ask.

SOME MAY ASK ...

> *"Did you ever worry that this situation could work
> out badly for Ben and Rachel?"*

TO YOU I SAY ...

> *"I have to be honest. I did wonder at first if it
> was fair to put these lovely people through this
> ordeal. Thankfully, however, it was their choice
> to move forward. When the time came to place
> the cherished baby in their arms, I trusted with
> all my heart that everything was going to work
> out according to God's plan."*

CHAPTER 13

Our time with Camille's little one was quickly coming to an end. During those hours in the hospital, our family had been through a wide spectrum of emotions. All who had met this sweet child had fallen in love with her. We had held her and hugged her; we had talked to her and cried over her. We had cherished each moment with her. I guess I should have known it would happen like that. Although we are far from perfect, our family has a great deal of love to share.

As much as we treasured the overwhelming joy surrounding this miracle of new life, we knew that it was transitional joy. Soon it would pass to others. I wanted to hold on to the feeling of intense love as long as I could. I could see that Camille was basking in maternal love, as well. As the hours passed, she held her baby close and spoke words of love to her. I'm sure Camille's voice was soothing to her little one. I know it was soothing to me.

I became increasingly aware that this child truly was a miracle, in every sense of the word. Among other things, she was a sign of God's love. She had brought healing to my beloved Camille, leading her on a path toward wholeness. I thanked God for that—*abundantly*. I prayed for Camille's baby as I had never prayed before. "Please, Lord," I begged, "place this child in loving arms and watch over her for the rest of her life. Keep her safe and healthy and happy, and please be with her parents—all of them."

In another part of the country, two very excited people were rushing to prepare for their journey to parenthood and a love they could not have imagined in their wildest dreams. Ben and Rachel knew they were heading into a complicated and potentially hurtful situation, yet they were willing to sacrifice anything to have this baby in their lives. With a clear understanding of the situation and a willingness to move forward, they headed our way.

While we waited for their arrival, my thoughts turned to David once again. What was going through his mind right now? Although he had not shared our loving and emotional experience at the hospital, he would soon meet his daughter. There was no doubt in my mind that he would immediately love this little child, just as we did. It was understandable that he would want her in his life; after all, she was his flesh and blood. Beyond that, attached to this baby was David's hope for a happy future with Camille.

Someone once said, "We do not see things as they are. We see them as *we* are." This is so true. While watching Camille with her baby, I thought about everyone who was now involved in the life of this child. Each of us saw the situation from his or her individual viewpoint, at this given place and time. In Camille's eyes, this baby deserved a stable home with two loving parents. Undoubtedly, this came from her personal experience in life. In the eyes of Ben and Rachel, this child was a miraculous answer to their prayers. This was surely born from the ashes of their previous sorrow and loss. David, too, saw the situation from his own perspective. Although he hadn't had much time to contemplate the big picture, David saw this child as an extension of himself and a possible fulfillment of his dream of a happy family. I thought back to my recent conversation with him about his own broken family, and I could understand why this vision was so important to him.

Becoming lost in my thoughts, I realized that I desperately needed to get grounded in God. This was all so complicated. I believed I understood how the situation was meant to evolve, but I acknowledged that there would be pain along the way. This was difficult to face. I cared very much about each of those involved. Again, I prayed to God. This time I asked him to protect the hearts that circled this child who, at this point, belonged only to him.

SOME MAY ASK ...

> *"You seem to care about David. Didn't you think it*
> *was admirable that he wanted to keep his baby?"*

TO YOU I SAY ...

> *"Yes, it was admirable. But each time my*
> *heart went out to David—and it often did—I*
> *remembered that the focus needed to be on the*
> *well-being of this vulnerable child. It was not her*
> *fault that she came into the world under these*
> *circumstances. She deserved to be given the best*
> *opportunities in life."*

Chapter 14

Earlier in the day, arrangements had been made to meet Ben and Rachel in the hospital chapel to give them Camille's baby—their baby. They would then stay in town until a meeting with David could be arranged. Paul, Camille, and I waited anxiously for their call to tell us they had arrived. The phone rang much too soon, and a new level of grief overcame the three of us. I found myself wanting to cry out, "Please, we can't do this!" Instead, I focused my attention on Camille. My dear Camille—I will never, *ever* forget the depth of pain in her eyes. I pray that I never see that look in my daughter's eyes again.

Paul was overcome with emotion as he gave the baby one last kiss. He quickly left the room to meet Ben and Rachel in the lobby. Certain that she could not take the baby to her new parents, Camille had asked me earlier to help her with this. Now, with steel in her voice, she was very clear about what she needed me to do. "Mom, when it's time to take my baby, I want you to go out that door and not turn back. I can only do this once." I agreed, knowing how difficult this was going to be for her. I left Camille alone to say her final goodbye to her little angel and paced the hall outside her door. When I heard her call, I went into the room and gently hugged the two of them.

Soon the little one was in my arms, and I headed toward the door. I was grateful for Camille's firm instructions not to turn back, because I never could have left her otherwise. The deep, sorrowful wailing I heard as I left the room was haunting. An echo of pure and intense pain, it was almost more than I could bear. I joined the baby's nurse in the hall, and we stepped into the elevator. I sobbed uncontrollably. During our fateful walk to the chapel, I assured the nurse that I was thankful the precious baby in my arms was going to have a good life with her new parents, but my heart was breaking for *my* baby back in that room.

I calmed myself down and struggled to focus on the task at hand. Paul had met the parents, and together they had gone to the chapel. It seemed like such a perfect setting for this transition to take place. After all, it was God who had made this possible. I will never forget the moment I entered that sacred space and saw the eager faces of those two beautiful young people—and Paul, whose face was drawn with sadness. It was all so bittersweet.

Before I knew it, I had kissed Camille's little angel for what I believed would be the last time, and I had placed her in her new mother's open arms. Everyone in the room, including the nurse, was crying. There were tears of joy mixed with tears of pain. I was reminded of the words I often cling to: *God never promised that life would be easy, but he promised to be with us in our joy and in our sorrow.* There was no doubt he was with us in the chapel that day.

Rachel held the baby close, and I remember thinking how wonderful it must feel to her to have a baby—*her* baby—in her arms after all the years of hoping and dreaming. She looked up at me through tears and said, "You have no idea how much this means." I smiled and answered that I understood; I had known the joy of having Camille placed in my arms years ago. I told Ben and Rachel that we knew God had chosen the perfect parents to raise this child. As I write these words today, in an effort to share that poignant conversation, I realize that words alone do not begin to convey the feelings of that moment. How could they?

I soon found myself thinking of Camille, alone in her room upstairs. Rachel must have somehow understood because she asked me how Camille was doing. It touched me that she was concerned about Camille in the midst of her own joy. I shared what we all knew to be true, that this was a difficult time for Camille. In spite of her original plans to stay disconnected, she had grown to love this baby very much, just as they would. I asked what they were going to name their daughter, and they said that she was going to be Emma. *Such a sweet name,* I thought. It would be nice to finally have a name to call her. I knew, however, that "Little Angel" had been the perfect name for her while she was with us.

SOME MAY ASK ...

> *"Did Camille ever talk to a counselor before the baby arrived or during the grieving process?"*

TO YOU I SAY ...

> *"While this experience would have been much easier for Camille with the support of a professional, she resisted the idea. The same young woman who wanted to go into childbirth 'cold turkey' wanted to deal with her emotional pain in her own way."*

CHAPTER 15

As Ben and Rachel gazed adoringly at their little treasure, Paul and I looked at each other with sadness in our eyes. We knew the time had come for us to say goodbye, so we reached out with warm hugs for this beautiful new family. It was a tender moment, one that will be etched in my mind forever.

We left the chapel and silently walked hand in hand to Camille's room. I was afraid to speak for fear I would completely break down. I thought to myself that this must truly be what a broken heart feels like. It was clear that Paul was feeling the same. Outside Camille's room, we held on to each other and tried to gather some much-needed strength.

When we walked though the door, we saw that Camille was dressed and ready to leave. There were no questions at that moment, although she would have many questions later. I could tell she was drained from the emotional experience of letting her baby go, not to mention the physical experience of the childbirth itself. She just wanted to go home. As the three of us walked down the hospital hall, Paul and I thanked everyone for their kindness and their care. These people were true professionals with hearts of gold. They had helped make this experience more positive than I ever could have imagined.

It was actually quite difficult to leave the hospital, although I had not expected it to be. I remember thinking that walking out those doors meant the beautiful experience we had shared was over. It was sad, but it was the reality. Camille had come to the hospital to bring a new life into the world, and she was now leaving empty-handed. I know she felt empty—I could see it in her eyes. The pain that Paul and I felt, great as it seemed, was nothing compared to hers. As we walked to the car and drove home on that balmy summer evening, no one said a word.

Those first few hours back at home were filled with great sadness—deep, deep sadness. Our hearts were heavy with grief; even the air felt heavy with grief. Somehow, and I thank God for this, I was able to find peace in the fact that little Emma was where she was meant to be. I found solace in the awareness that her adoptive parents had been richly blessed. This gave me the strength to be fully attentive to Camille, who was experiencing terribly intense feelings.

It was at this time that she asked me to tell her about the new parents and describe what it had been like in that little chapel. We talked for a long time, neither of us ready to face the silent void that the night would bring. Camille spoke openly about how she was feeling, and I saw this as a gift—certainly for me, but especially for Camille as her healing began. At the end of the evening, Camille came over and sat on my lap like she did when she was a child. She sobbed on my shoulder well into the night.

Over the next few days, Camille ached intensely for her baby. I had never seen her shed so many tears. While it was difficult to see her in such pain, I knew the tears were an important part of her grieving. Many times she said to me, "Mom, if I could only hold her one more time." Each time she said this, I held her close and gently told her that one more time would never be enough. I promised her that each day would be a little easier, and I prayed that God would make it so. After all, he was still very present in this situation, and he was still doing the work of the great choreographer.

It is important to reiterate here that in the days before Emma's birth, Camille had rejected the idea of an open adoption which would have allowed her to be part of her baby's life. I understood completely why she had made that choice. It was a protective decision to make everything easier for her in the future. The harsh reality of that decision, now that Emma was with her new parents, was that we would never see her again. There would be no "one more time." We struggled to accept that reality.

As a mother, it was natural for me to focus on Camille and her needs. I kept telling myself that this was not about me. However, the truth of the matter was that I could not deny the personal pain I was feeling. I had watched as my darling granddaughter entered the world, and I had instantly been blessed with a grandmother's love. While it

~ ❧ ~

was an amazing privilege to be part of God's plan and place Camille's child in the arms of her new mother, it didn't make the feeling of grandmother go away. I knew I was going to have to work hard to overcome my own grief, separate from Camille. It wasn't going to be easy.

SOME MAY ASK ...

> *"It seems as if the birth father—and his resistance to his child's adoption—should have been more of a concern during this time, yet he is hardly mentioned. Why is that?"*

TO YOU I SAY ...

> *"At this point in the journey, it does appear that David's presence was ignored. I apologize if it seems disrespectful to David; that would never be my intention. The reality is that there was always an underlying anxiety about the issue of Emma's birth father. It was a huge issue, of course, but it seemed to take a backseat to the various emotions that everyone was experiencing with Emma's arrival. Did we have blinders on as we moved forward with Camille's plan for adoption? Perhaps. All I know is that each of us clung to the hope that everything would work out in the best way for all involved. On a personal level, I clung desperately to my faith that God would make everything right."*

CHAPTER 16

Unfamiliar with the legal aspects surrounding the situation with Emma, we placed our trust in Christine. As the attorney for Camille and her baby in the adoption process, Christine was the contact person between Camille and Ben and Rachel, who were encouraged to procure their own attorney. Christine communicated with the adoptive parents and continued to be in close contact with Camille. A loving and sensitive person, Christine soon became very special to us.

We were aware that Ben and Rachel were staying across town those first few days, getting to know little Emma and waiting for the meeting David had requested. Christine had been painstakingly honest about David's rights as the birth father, and we all knew that he had the power to eventually take Emma from Ben and Rachel and raise her on his own. This was a frightening realization. As the meeting time approached, we could only hope he had done some serious soul searching—beyond simply hoping for a renewed relationship with Camille—and could see that he was not prepared to give this child what she deserved.

I am choosing not to dwell on those reasons why David wasn't prepared at this point in time to be a father. To do so would be unfair to him. I believe there is goodness in each of us, and certainly there is goodness in David; this would become clear to me in the months ahead. However, it takes more than goodness to give a child what is needed to grow up in this world. It takes a great deal of maturity, stability, and commitment—among other things. Ideally, those who choose to have children are equipped for the often-challenging task. Admittedly, Camille was not. There were many who agreed that David was not either.

When the time came for David to meet his daughter, we wondered how the fragile situation was going to play out. It would be a significant moment, to be sure. I was constantly in prayer that morning, knowing that God would be present at the meeting too. I asked him to bless each of those who were united by this child. I prayed for wisdom and understanding on everyone's part. I prayed for openness to his will, whatever that might be. "Above all," I prayed, "let goodness prevail."

Christine immediately called Camille after the meeting, as she had promised she would. She shared that David had been very respectful to Ben and Rachel, which eventually put everyone at ease. Upon meeting the couple and his child, David seemed content to look at little Emma in Rachel's arms and watch her from where he sat across the room. At one point, he took pictures of Emma with his cell phone. During the initial awkward moments, Ben and Rachel did their best to carry on a casual conversation with David, sincerely wanting to learn more about him. They shared openly about themselves, as well, desperately hoping that he would accept them—perhaps even accept them as adoptive parents for his daughter.

A more deliberate discussion followed. Once again, the need for an official paternity test was discussed, and David said he would take care of it immediately. Christine explained to David that the results of the test wouldn't be known for a couple of weeks. While acknowledging that his permission wasn't required, she thanked him for allowing Emma to go home with Ben and Rachel, rather than wait those two weeks in a strange town. It was important to Camille, Christine told him, and it was important for Emma, too.

Ben and Rachel were relieved that the meeting was going so well. Everyone seemed to be calm and cooperative. Yet it soon became clear that this had been the easy part of the discussion; the rest was going to be much more difficult to face. When the tender subject of adoption was brought up, David abruptly announced that Emma was his daughter, and he was going to raise her. He then got up and walked out of the office, leaving behind the devastated young couple—and his baby. He had never even asked to hold her.

SOME MAY ASK ...

> *"What went through your mind when you were told that David was unyielding in his plan to keep his baby?"*

TO YOU I SAY ...

> *"I cannot begin to describe the concern I had for Emma when I heard those words, nor the devastation I felt for Ben and Rachel. This was one of many prayerful moments when I turned to God in complete surrender."*

CHAPTER 17

Although news of David's announcement elicited anger on Camille's part, we didn't fully comprehend the power behind his words. Honestly, we didn't see how it could possibly be. Surely there was some set of standards that had to be met; certainly someone would be able to intervene and confirm that David didn't have the necessary qualifications to raise Emma. In our naiveté and self-imposed denial, we saw this as a temporary setback, one we assumed would quickly be resolved.

At this point, Camille and I still believed we would never see Emma again. Although I honored her grief, I kept hoping the days ahead would become easier for my hurting daughter. I suggested that it might be healing to put together a little box for the baby and her parents. Camille seemed to like the idea. We thought it might affirm to Ben and Rachel that we had faith everything was going to work out with the adoption, as planned. Before moving ahead, however, Camille called Christine and asked her to check with the parents to make sure this was something they would like. She wanted to be respectful of their feelings, especially now that they were living with uncertainty.

Christine thought it was a fine idea. She soon reported back to us that she had spoken with Ben and Rachel, and they had assured her they would love to hear from us. Christine also shared that the parents were anxious about the situation with David, but little Emma was doing well and they adored her beyond words. I believe this communication via Christine was, for all concerned, like a soothing salve on an open wound. Looking back, I can see that God's handiwork was again at play, beginning to unite two families that would soon become one.

Camille and I set out to fill the "love box" for the new family. The project brought some much-needed joy to our hearts. Camille chose a darling pink outfit with the words *little angel* on the front and selected some other sweet baby girl items, as well. I dug into my boxes of pictures (always waiting to be put into albums!) and found my favorite pictures of Camille when she was young. I thought that perhaps Ben and Rachel might like to see the resemblance, if there was any, as Emma grew up. I made a collage of current pictures of our family, including a grown-up Camille and her sisters, Paul and me, and the family pup. On her own, Camille wrote a letter from the depth of her heart and tucked it inside. I knew this was an important thing for her to do—for many reasons.

There were words that I, too, needed to share with Emma's new parents—for different reasons. As I sat down to write, the words flowed from my heart.

Dear Ben and Rachel,

I will forever be in awe of the miracle of your little Emma. From the moment I discovered there was a baby on the way, I knew that God was going to make everything work out just as it was meant to be, according to his plan. I knew he had already picked out the baby's parents, and I was so eager to know who you were.

As Emma's arrival day grew near and we learned about you, Camille was certain you were meant to be Emma's parents. In her certainty and in my faith, I found great comfort in knowing that you were the parents God had chosen. We have heard such wonderful things about you both! Our family is so thankful that Emma will spend the rest of her life with such caring, loving people.

In the two short days she was with us, your little angel left such an imprint on our hearts. I saw beautiful healing take place in the heart of my Camille as she discovered a depth of love she had never known possible. And I saw such strength in her character as she stayed committed to doing what she knew was right for her baby. During those hours of joy and tears, she never faltered in knowing that Emma belonged to you. I am so proud of her.

Upon meeting both of you, it was clear to me why you were chosen to be Emma's parents. As I placed her in your arms, Rachel, I could feel the love that waited for her, and I saw it in your face as well, Ben. As difficult as it was, I knew this was meant to be.

Please know that your family will always be in our thoughts and prayers. We often think of you and imagine the happiness you share. Emma has brought us great happiness, too, and we are thankful for the time that she blessed Camille and our family with her love. That love will never go away …

We send love and God's blessings to you all,

Grace

SOME MAY ASK …

"Did you expect to hear from Ben and Rachel after they received the package and the letters?"

TO YOU I SAY …

"I honestly did not. Our intention was to share 'a bit of us' with the new parents and offer them love and support. This helped to ease Camille's pain, and that was enough for me. I did not need more."

CHAPTER 18

After we sent the package off in the mail, Camille and I felt a wonderful sense of peace. We wondered out loud what their reaction would be when they opened the box. Would it mean as much to them to receive those items as it had meant to us to gather and send them? We didn't expect to ever know. As the tenuous situation with David began to unfold, however, we soon discovered that what we had assumed was a closing chapter in the story of Camille's little angel was actually the beginning chapter—of a long, involved journey that would weave in and out of joy and despair.

Camille knew the paternity test would show that David was Emma's biological father, so it was no surprise when Christine called two weeks later to give us that information. After speaking with Camille, Christine called David to give him the results, as well. David repeated to Christine that he intended to raise Emma. Once again, he said he hoped the baby would establish a connection between him and Camille. "Camille's going to have to deal with me if I raise our child," he told Christine.

From their previous conversations, Christine was well aware that Camille had no intention of simply handing Emma over to David. Camille was adamant that this was not best for Emma, and she was willing to fight for what she thought was right. Christine explained this to David. She told him to anticipate a lengthy and involved procedure in the months ahead, and she advised him to get an attorney to represent him. Christine also stressed that it would be in Emma's best interest to leave her settled in her present home as the process began. At the first court hearing, Christine told David, the judge would determine where Emma would live during the process. Thankfully, David agreed to continue with the current arrangement.

In a follow-up conversation with Camille, Christine explained what had been said. She told Camille that David had agreed to allow Emma to stay with Ben and Rachel for the time being. She went on to say that while she would be able to represent Camille and Emma in the adoption process—if there was going to be an adoption process—it was now necessary for Camille to work with an attorney who specialized in more complicated cases. She gave Camille the names of two attorneys. Christine mentioned that she had worked with one of the attorneys and had a great deal of respect for him, as did the legal community in our town. The other lawyer was a woman Christine knew only through her reputation as a strong attorney.

Camille's spirit was becoming stronger each day, and she had a great deal of fight in her at this point. While she had no idea what needed to be done, she was ready to move forward quickly to ensure that Emma would be able to stay with Ben and Rachel forever. Camille immediately called the attorney with whom Christine had worked and was told by his secretary that he didn't have an opening until the following week. That wasn't soon enough for Camille; she quickly called the other attorney's office. The woman could see Camille the following day. It seemed like a blessing at the time.

Let me stress here that, from start to finish, I was involved in Emma's legal situation only as much as Camille asked me to be. I say this because it was very clear the attorney we saw the next day was not happy that I had accompanied Camille to the appointment. I want to give the lawyer the benefit of the doubt and assume that my presence was responsible for the extremely negative tone that permeated the entire visit. It was quite an intense hour, to say the least, and Camille and I were shocked by her demeanor. The attorney began by saying that she had personally been in the exact situation Camille was now in. Although it had eventually worked out positively for her, it had been very difficult. She told Camille that she just needed to let Emma go.

It sounded to us like a mixed message, given the attorney's own experience, but that was beside the point. We had expected honesty, yet we were also under the impression that a legal counselor would offer possible options. While Camille's main concern was the well-being of her daughter, she also cared about the couple who was prepared to be the child's parents. This didn't seem important to the attorney, however. She harshly told Camille, "They're not your problem."

As I look back on this, I am still stunned by the animosity and sense of hopelessness presented to Camille on that summer afternoon. It was sunny and beautiful when we walked out of the building, but our hearts felt only darkness and despair. I remember thinking, *If ever there was a time for prayer, it is now.* Unfortunately, I was too numb to find the words to share with God.

SOME MAY ASK ...

> *"Were you angry at the harsh words of the attorney?"*

TO YOU I SAY ...

> *"I wouldn't say that I felt anger. I was surprised by what she said to us, and I was shocked at the way she chose to say it. Once again, however, I was reminded that we all bring 'who we are' to various situations in our lives, and ultimately this colors our attitudes and our actions."*

CHAPTER 19

Our spirits were shattered after the bleak conversation with the attorney, but we soon regained our focus: Emma. I had the advantage of my faith in God's goodness and my belief in his holy plan to get me back on track; Camille did not. I write those last words cautiously, for fear that it gives the impression that my belief system sets me higher or makes me better. Nothing could be further from my personal truth.

From as early as I can remember, my faith in God has always been an integral part of me. It is not due to any religion, although I have certainly appreciated many aspects of religion in my life. It's much more. It's a deep spirituality on which I rely heavily. Faith is not something that someone gives you, or I would certainly have given it to Camille. I know from experience that my life seems much easier when I'm able to surrender my fears to God. As we faced the various challenges on this journey, I relied on my God and Camille relied on me. In my heart, I knew God was guiding us both. I point this out now because we were about to run into a huge wall.

Camille was extremely discouraged after our meeting with the attorney. In addition to her feelings of discouragement, she was experiencing some expected postpartum depression. I remember well the afternoon of her follow-up obstetric appointment. We were sitting under a shade tree outside the doctor's office while she waited to go inside.

Camille was especially sad that day. So much had happened in such a short time. She now realized the fight to carry out her dream for Emma was going to involve more than she felt capable of giving, especially in her current state of mind. She told me that she knew David was incapable of giving Emma what a child needed in life, but she didn't have the strength to fight for the adoption—and she certainly didn't have the strength to raise a child. Camille was conflicted and weary. I remember telling her that she needed to have faith, but that was a mistake. Her response was, "That's *your* thing, Mom, not mine."

Well, it *was* "my thing" and it guided me through the next difficult moments. In one of our most poignant conversations ever, I told Camille I loved her more than she would ever know. I reminded her that I had willingly fought for her every moment of her life with us, through some very challenging times. Looking deep into her eyes, I said that now it was time for her to fight—for *her* daughter. If the adoption was not meant to be, we would know. As far as I could tell, however, this is exactly how it was meant to be. There was no response. As Camille left me to go to her appointment, we were both in tears.

As if this moment wasn't difficult enough, my cell phone soon began to ring. I looked at the incoming call and saw that it was Rachel. My heart stopped. I hadn't spoken with her since that day in the hospital chapel when I placed Emma in her arms. I answered the phone and greeted her warmly, but cautiously. After our initial hellos, Rachel told me that she and Emma were in town.

Rachel explained that when Christine had contacted her and Ben to pass on the results of the paternity test, she had encouraged them to hire an attorney because the situation was becoming very complex. From the sound of Christine's voice, Ben and Rachel understood the gravity of the picture. They immediately made the decision for Rachel to come back to town and live here with Emma until the adoption issues were resolved. It was important to them to make sure everything was legal. These new parents had every intention of fighting for their child, and they were under the impression that Camille was also willing to fight. They were under that impression because Camille had previously committed to it, but now …

Rachel went on to tell me how much they adored their little girl and said they were terrified of losing her. Megan, Rachel's aunt, had made the trip with mom and baby to offer emotional support and help with Emma, whom their entire family had grown to love. Although they were aunt and niece, Megan and Rachel were close in age and close in spirit, as well. I was thankful that Rachel had the support she needed. She told me where they were staying and said they were prepared to make this their home as long as necessary. We made arrangements to meet that afternoon at a nearby park. After I hung up the phone, I prayed with all my heart that Camille's strength and commitment would be renewed.

SOME MAY ASK ...

> *"What were you going to do if Camille refused*
> *to follow through with her plans to fight for the*
> *adoption?"*

TO YOU I SAY ...

> *"I honestly did not know. Many thoughts raced*
> *through my mind in that instant. Thankfully,*
> *God quieted those thoughts as quickly as they*
> *appeared."*

CHAPTER 20

By the time Camille returned to the car after her appointment, we had both calmed down. I had done my best to put things in perspective, without all the emotion that had stirred our earlier conversation. Camille had been given a clean bill of health and was feeling stronger, physically *and* emotionally. I told her about the phone call from Rachel. If she was willing, I explained, plans were in place to meet at the park. The anticipation of seeing Emma again and meeting Rachel for the first time clearly brought a wave of joy to Camille.

I didn't attempt to revisit the conversation we had shared earlier, hoping that perhaps Camille would change her mind about fighting for the adoption once she saw Emma again. I had a sense that things were going to be different after this reunion. Surprisingly, Camille brought up the topic herself. Although she was dreading the challenge before her, she had already decided that she was not willing to give up on Emma's adoption. Prayers had been answered—again.

I could hardly wait to call Paul. "You'll never guess who Camille and I are going to meet at the park!" I cried out. To say he was surprised would be an understatement, but then there were many surprises along this journey. To be honest, Paul didn't share my belief that everything was going to work out as we hoped it would. While he is a man of strong faith, Paul often has a pragmatic way of looking at things. I call him my "voice of reason". After hearing the attorney's negative message, Paul had immediately begun to prepare Camille and me for the painful situation that was looming. He went into his protective mode—for Camille's heart, for my heart, and for his. At this moment, however, Paul gave us his blessing and said to give Rachel and the baby a hug.

With that blessing, Camille and I headed to the park. This day was certainly turning out to be different than it had begun! Unaware of what lay ahead, I thanked God for his intervention and prayed that he would be with Camille and Rachel as they met for the first time. And I prayed for sweet little Emma.

It was a lovely day as we drove into the park. The sky was a beautiful blue with fluffy white clouds. All around us, children laughed and played joyfully. Ducks swam in the pond, and beautiful white swans floated nearby. Their quiet serenity brought a sense of calm to my racing heart.

I looked at Camille to see how she was feeling. It was clear from her face that she had a multitude of emotions vying for her attention. It was the same look I had seen as she held her baby in the hospital. I couldn't even imagine what was going through her mind. Her plea to hold her little angel one more time was about to be answered. And soon, very soon, she was going to meet the mother God had chosen for that little angel. It felt like one of life's mystical moments.

The two of us watched as Rachel and Megan drove into the lot and parked next to us. Rachel quickly got out of the car and walked toward us. It felt to me like a beautiful, though unexpected, reunion with someone who had special meaning in my life. She and I exchanged hugs, and she introduced her aunt to us. Then, in the warm sunlight of that afternoon, everything seemed to stand still as Rachel looked at Camille and Camille looked at Rachel.

Words cannot begin to describe the depth of their gazes. There was overwhelming gratitude and compassion on Rachel's face. Camille's face showed a fragile uncertainty, as if she was fighting back strong emotions that she didn't want to spill out. I also saw on my daughter's beautiful face a sense of relief that this moment had, against all odds, arrived. I will tell you this: it was a privilege to be present at that moment. It had significant spiritual meaning for me. I looked at Megan, whom I did not even know, and I could tell that she felt the same.

Rachel broke the silence by asking Camille if she wanted to hold Emma. I was touched by the obvious significance of that kind gesture. I could tell it was very important to Rachel that Camille be given the chance to hold her baby right away; it was a beautiful, sincere offering. Camille immediately said

~ 🦋 ~

yes and waited eagerly while Rachel unbuckled the small bundle. As Rachel placed a sleeping Emma into Camille's arms, I watched my daughter fall in love all over again. I prayed that this would be a good thing.

Some may ask ...

> "*Was there concern that this new development may lead to disaster?*"

To you I say ...

> "*At this specific moment in time, it seemed as if everything was unfolding beautifully—with spiritual guidance. When things happen peacefully, I can feel God's presence. This was one of those occasions.*"

CHAPTER 21

During our time at the park, with its many tender moments, it felt as if we had all known each other for a very long time. I was especially touched by something Megan said when we were leaving to go our separate ways. As we hugged each other goodbye and vowed to meet again soon, I told Rachel and Megan how thankful we were that Emma was with such a wonderful family. Megan took my hands in hers and said, "Grace, we are *all* family." How right she was!

As Camille and I left, I thought about how things had changed. Just a few weeks before, Camille was aching to hold her baby, certain that she would never see her again. The upheaval we faced with David's decision was upsetting, to say the least, but many blessings had arisen from this new situation. Two families had now come together, united by their love for a special child, and nothing was ever going to be the same. I never could have imagined this was possible. I remember offering a prayer of praise, as I often do: "God, you are unbelievably good!"

It was not long before Camille and I met again with Rachel and Megan and sweet Emma. Rachel was eager to know the current status of the situation, so Camille brought her up-to-date on the specifics of the meeting with the attorney. Seeing the fear in their eyes, Camille did her best to reassure Rachel and Megan. She said Christine spoke very highly of Phillip B., the other attorney she had suggested. Christine had worked with him personally and knew him to be a wise and well-respected lawyer; she had encouraged Camille to talk with him as soon as possible. I was proud to hear Camille tell Rachel that she would call him the next day. After holding little Emma once again and seeing how much the little one meant to these fine people, Camille's passion had returned.

Within a matter of days, Camille met with Phillip while Rachel, Megan, and I played with Emma in his waiting room. It was apparent on the first visit that he was truly a professional, in every sense of the word. During their conversation, Camille later shared, she was completely honest with Phillip about the situation and told him exactly what she hoped for. He listened calmly. When Camille had finished, Phillip simply said that it was going to be an interesting case. He did not seem fazed in the least.

After he had spoken at length with Camille, he asked the rest of us to join them with any questions we might have. Once he explained what he had shared with Camille, I had no questions at all. What I did have was instant respect and trust. Phillip appeared to be everything that

Christine had said he was: knowledgeable, ethical, wise, and kind.

Phillip explained to all of us that if David chose to fight for custody of Emma, which was his right, the potential adoption would be placed on the back burner. The legal process would begin at square one with the issue of temporary custody. There would be an initial court hearing to determine which parent, Camille or David, would be awarded temporary custody of Emma. Phillip felt confident that Camille would be awarded initial custody, as the court usually favored the mother. At some point, evaluations would be done on both parents to determine that each was fit to raise Emma. There would be other court hearings at various intervals to revisit the custody decision and look at Emma's well-being, which, of course, was the main focus of the court.

Phillip gave us encouragement when he told us that many birth fathers who seek custody give up when they see how long and drawn out the process is, what it entails, and what it costs in attorney's fees. They also become discouraged once they have a complete understanding of what it takes to raise a child, financially and otherwise. We hoped this would be the situation with David.

It all sounded so cut and dried, yet we knew we were walking on a rocky path. This was not going to be an easy journey, but at least we had strong legal guidance. All of us—Camille, Paul and I, and Ben and Rachel and their families—felt relieved that Camille had a good attorney to represent her. While we understood that this was the beginning of a long and complicated process, we were thankful to be moving forward.

SOME MAY ASK ...

> *"You talk about custody issues between Camille and David, but where does the adoption fit in?"*

TO YOU I SAY ...

> *"Temporary custody was just the beginning step of a process that we hoped would result in Emma's adoption. As Phillip explained, it was important to honor David's rights in the eyes of the law. Camille made the decision to fight for initial custody of Emma at this point because she was not willing to consider the alternative, which was to relinquish Emma to David. We needed to be patient and trust. We needed to continue to pray."*

CHAPTER 22

And so it was that we took a new path on this miraculous adventure. While we waited to hear if David had retained his own attorney and was, indeed, going to seek custody of Emma, life seemed to be in a peaceful limbo. No news was good news, as far as we were concerned. Megan returned home to her family, and Rachel settled in with little Emma. She tried to put her fears and anxiety behind her and enjoy the new surroundings. Ben remained at their home far away, working at his jobs and missing his girls terribly.

Camille returned to work and tried to regain a sense of normalcy that had been uprooted for almost a year. While she was the in-charge person regarding the situation with Emma, she relied heavily on Paul and me for support. As for us, Paul and I did our best to pick up where we had left off before all of this began. I completed my last round of chemotherapy and was given the oh-so-welcome news that the treatments had been successful. My cancer was in remission.

While we were thankful to be connected with Emma and her family—and we were *very* thankful—Camille and I knew it was important to be respectful of their situation. We didn't want to be intrusive in their lives in any way, so we were cautious. It was much like walking a tightrope. The situation was challenging for them, as well. Rachel was on her own in a strange town, going about her new life with Emma, yet aware that this new life was hanging in the boughs with the baby, so to speak. It seemed like a delicate balance for everyone, but I think all of us would agree that we balanced it well.

As we waited to see if David had changed his mind, I found myself in the (self-imposed, as usual) position of cheerleader for Ben and Rachel, as well as Camille. It's just what I do. But there came a time when I needed a support system myself. I told Camille I wanted to share what was going on in my life with my closest friends—my spiritual sisters, as I call them. I wanted to be able to show them pictures and perhaps even have them meet little Emma and Ben and Rachel in the future. Above all, I really needed their prayers—we all did! Camille knew these women well, as they had always been a special part of my life, and she felt close to them, too. She said, "I understand, Mom," and went on to tell me that she would actually welcome their support. I was excited, but I knew the time had to be right to share Emma's story.

Although it was actually only a few weeks, it seemed like quite a bit of time passed before the call came to tell

Camille that David had hired an attorney and was starting proceedings to gain custody of Emma. The first court date was scheduled for the distant future. The process had begun, but we could see that it was not going to be a speedy process. I was certain, however, that God was going to be with us each and every moment.

Many more weeks went by before the court date finally arrived. (To our surprise, David did not ask to see his daughter at all during that time.) As Phillip had predicted, the initial court hearing resulted in Camille officially, though temporarily, obtaining custody of Emma. At Phillip's request, David was ordered to pay child support each month. At the request of David and his attorney, he was given visitation rights. After a bit of discussion between the attorneys, and agreement on everyone's part, it was determined that the three weekly visits would be supervised visits in our home.

Camille and I left the courtroom elated at the results and eager to share the news with Rachel, who was anxiously waiting to hear from Camille. The decision regarding visitation was going to present some new challenges, but I knew it was only fair that David be allowed to see his daughter. What I did not know was how meaningful those visits would be and how conflicted I would become as I watched the relationship between Emma and her birth father develop. I would need to rely on my faith in God's plan now more than ever.

SOME MAY ASK ...

> *"Did the judge know that Camille had made an earlier decision to give Emma up for adoption?"*

TO YOU I SAY ...

> *"Yes, he did. David's attorney presented this fact at the beginning of the hearing. Phillip simply responded that Camille had initially felt this was best for the baby. At this time, however, it was her desire to be given custody of Emma. I was surprised and grateful that this was actually a 'non-issue' at the hearing. I really do believe the judge had Emma's best interest in mind every step of the way."*

CHAPTER 23

When Camille was given temporary custody of Emma, it became clear that God's plan had taken a turn—in our eyes, but not his, of course. I believed he knew what was going to take place each step of the way. However, I also believed we needed to make good choices in what we said and did, and we needed to strive to be our best selves. Thankfully, this did not seem to be difficult for any of us. We had become a team that relied on each other for the good of this child.

What did it mean that Camille had temporary custody of Emma? In the eyes of the law, it was presumed that Emma would be in her care. To Camille, it meant Emma would also be in the care of Ben and Rachel, who had been with her since she was one day old. Camille remained adamant that Emma would have a stable beginning in her life, yet we needed to honor the expectations of the court. So we did what seemed like the only possible thing to do: we invited Rachel and Emma, and Ben when he came to visit, to live with us.

I am aware that many will question how we were able to make this gesture, knowing we were becoming extremely attached to these people and would be saying goodbye again in the future. For those of us living in the midst of the situation, however, it seemed like a natural step. At this point, we were already deeply connected to Emma and her parents, and there was no turning back. We were all beginning to feel like an extended family, brought together for a very important purpose.

We began to make changes in our lives to accommodate the situation that we believed would lead to Emma's adoption. None of us had any idea how long the process was going to take, so we simply moved forward in faith. Paul and I set up a spare bedroom in our home. It was already painted pink, which made me smile, and a collection of angels added a loving touch. We did everything we could to make the room comfortable and cozy. We wanted this new family to feel completely at home.

It was lovely to have Rachel and Emma with us, and we looked forward to visits from Ben, as well. Camille and Sadie, our youngest daughter, and Paul and I were terribly excited to come home each day because we knew that little Emma would be there. While Beth lived too far away to come for a visit, Rebecca, who lived nearby, often stopped by to share in the joy of Emma. We all enjoyed this opportunity to get to know each other better.

One day, out of the blue, Rachel announced that she and Ben would like Emma to call me GG, for Grandma Grace.

After all my earlier efforts to suppress my grandmotherly instincts, I realized that Rachel was giving me permission to be Grandma. And so I became GG. Although it was too soon for Emma to say it, I loved hearing the rest of the family, including Ben and Rachel, call me by that name. Paul became GoGo, a funny little name that has no specific meaning. Rachel laughed when she told us, "I know it sounds silly, but it goes well with GG." We all loved it! It didn't sound silly to us at all, not then and not now. It's amazing how an affectionate name, assigned from two generous hearts, can bring such joy.

Rachel was very thoughtful about letting us hold Emma or give her a bottle. How I loved those tender times! Without even thinking about it, all of us fell into a nice rhythm. We helped out with Emma in whatever way we could, but we were careful not to overstep boundaries. In our minds, Emma belonged to Ben and Rachel, and we appreciated every moment we had with her and with them. We were thankful that they never seemed to feel uncomfortable or threatened by the situation.

It was so wonderful having a baby in the house, with all of the precious little sounds and the soft caresses. I spent many quiet moments gazing at Emma and feeling such awe at what was happening in our lives. How could this be? The flow of happiness I felt was such a gift, an unexpected and amazing gift. I could never have dreamed that Emma would be in our lives; I would never have even thought to pray for such a thing. At these moments, I remember thinking that this is what I love about my God. In his infinite wisdom, he can make our lives more wonderful than we could even imagine.

SOME MAY ASK ...

> *"What did Ben and Rachel select as Emma's name for Camille?"*

TO YOU I SAY ...

> *"Ever sensitive to her wishes, Rachel asked Camille what she would like Emma to call her. Camille said she needed some time to think about it. To this day, Camille has not chosen a special name for Emma to call her, and we all respect that. Emma calls her 'Camille,' and that seems to work well for both."*

CHAPTER 24

Soon we had settled into our new life. With Camille's permission, my dearest friends and many of our immediate family members were told about Emma. Since the baby and her parents were now living in our home, there was no way to keep it a secret from frequent visitors. Camille learned to be comfortable with this, once she felt the love that flowed from those who cared about her. However, there were still many who were not told Emma's story, at Camille's request, and do not know her story to this day.

Camille struggled daily to hold her emotions at bay. She needed to protect her heart, which had broken that day in the hospital and would surely break again when the adoption took place. Likewise, she felt the need to control her emotions because, like it or not, the weight of the situation rested on her shoulders at this point. As custodial parent, she was seen as the responsible party. She left the parenting piece to Ben and Rachel, but Camille was the one who had to jump through the legal hoops. She had to work with her attorney and attend the court hearings. She had to take the required classes and, most challenging of all, she had to deal with David.

After the initial court hearing, David began coming to the house three days a week for two hours at a time. The court had recommended these hours to allow him to get to know Emma and, hopefully, to bond with her. While I was to be the required supervision during those visits, there were still times that Camille needed to communicate with David. This was challenging for her, to say the least. Gone was the softness of heart that Emma's birth had created in her. Camille was now in the role of mother tiger looking out for her cub.

Each of us dreaded David's visits at first. Camille was anxious and resented having him in our home. The first time she handed Emma to him was extremely difficult for her. She soon found it was better if she was not home when he came. Camille's anxiety, however, was nothing compared to that of Ben and Rachel, who also left the house for his visits. They saw David as a threat to the adoption—which, of course, he was. I could see they shared a sense of compassion for David, but it was overshadowed by their intense fear of losing Emma. I understood. It was important to me, however, that Emma was not burdened with the negative feelings that were initially brought on by the visits. She did not deserve that. For that matter, neither did David.

Once we made it through the first week, the anxiety surrounding the visits seemed to lessen significantly, and a healthy pattern began to develop. David always arrived on time for each visit. We chatted for a few moments ("How are you doing?" "Emma smiled yesterday!" "It's getting cold, isn't it?") and then I placed Emma in his arms. As far as I was concerned, this was *his* special time. For the next two hours, David held Emma and watched her and talked to her in the comfort of our living room. Paul and I stayed in the nearby kitchen and family room, giving them space and privacy. Although I was always aware, I didn't want to intrude upon their time together.

Before long, I began to appreciate the sacredness of these visits. Please understand that my commitment to Emma's adoption never wavered. Ben and Rachel were excellent parents who loved her with all their hearts, and each day I could see the three of them developing a stronger sense of family. No, I didn't doubt for a moment that they were meant to be Emma's parents.

Yet there was an amazing dynamic developing during David's visits. He was clearly falling in love with Emma, just as the rest of us had. And she was responding to his love, just as she responded to all the love that was poured on her. Those visits, very simply put, were all about love. I found myself thanking God for this abundance of love that was blessing our family and our home. And I wondered, "How in the world—God's world—is this going to turn out?"

SOME MAY ASK …

> *"What were you feeling as you watched David become increasingly close to his daughter?"*

TO YOU I SAY …

> *"Again, I have to be honest. I was overwhelmed by the love that was developing. I had not expected this. In my mind, and in the minds of others, David was not prepared to offer this child what she needed in life. If we measure by stability and maturity and financial capabilities, this was true. But I saw that David was prepared to love his child, and we must never underestimate the power of love. This was a message I needed to learn. How did I feel? I was conflicted and confused."*

CHAPTER 25

By now Emma was more than four months old. She was a beautiful baby, a happy baby. Her smiles melted my heart. In those special moments when I held her in my arms and looked down at her sweet little face, her eyes seemed to reach into my soul. Those eyes radiated warmth—and something more. As I rocked her quietly one day, I recalled a theory I had read some time ago that suggested that each baby, together with God, picks his or her parents before coming to this life. I thought about this possibility as I gazed into Emma's eyes.

There was no doubt in my mind that Emma was heaven-sent. As I considered what I had read, I wondered if she and God together had picked Camille to be her birth mother. I had seen the blessings of Emma's birth; I knew in my heart those blessings were part of God's plan for Camille. And I would always believe that Ben and Rachel had been chosen by God to be her parents. If I accepted this, I had to accept that David, too, had been chosen to be part of this complicated picture. I wanted to believe there would be blessings for him from this situation, just as there had been blessings for Camille and all of us.

No one would have guessed from looking at Emma that her little life was in limbo. Ben and Rachel were absolutely devoted to her; they lived and breathed for this child. All of our family adored her *and* her wonderful parents. Her birth father cherished her, as well. She was in a home filled with love, and she was at the center. It would follow to say that life was good. For Camille and our family, it was. I suspect that David would even say that his life was good at this point, for he was enjoying time with his daughter and saw this as a step toward getting custody of her. But for Ben and Rachel, life was difficult.

Not that these two faithful people ever complained. They were increasingly thankful to have the gift of Emma in their lives, and they were clearly true to their commitment to sacrifice anything to keep her as their own. As the months passed, they made many sacrifices.

Ben had a very understanding boss, who often allowed him to travel the long distance back and forth between our home and theirs. But he also had a separate business of his own that he was trying to get up and running, and I could tell this was challenging. Whenever Ben was able to be with his family, he worked hard to squeeze in time for business while also enjoying precious time with his daughter and wife. He was stretched very thin.

Likewise, Rachel was doing her best to hold things together on their home front far away. Any problem that arose while they were both with us had to be taken care of from a distance. This was not easy. When Ben was back home and working his two jobs, he had no time to keep household things in order the way Rachel would have. In addition, Rachel was not able to return to work, which meant a significant decrease in their income. It was clear that this was a trying situation, as far as the nuts and bolts of life were concerned.

I could also see that Rachel was lonesome for her family and friends back home. Earlier, these people had sent Rachel and Emma off with their blessings and prayers, expecting that the new family would soon return to begin life together with all of them. Now these many months had passed with no sight of a happy ending, and family and friends were beginning to worry. Was this situation really going to turn out as everyone hoped? Or were Ben and Rachel in for the disappointment of their lives? It broke my heart to hear from Rachel that someone close to her had suggested it would be better to walk away from the fight for Emma and return home to their life without her.

At this point, I couldn't allow myself to even imagine what it would be like if this situation didn't end in Emma's adoption. Fear crept in at times, but I did my best to remain strong in my faith that the adoption was meant to be. I have to admit, though, that there were weak moments when I worried about everyone involved—especially Ben and Rachel.

SOME MAY ASK …

> *"Was there ever an alternative plan if David did not give up his fight for Emma?"*

TO YOU I SAY …

> *"A dear friend asked me if we had an alternative plan, out of concern that we may be setting ourselves up for deep heartache. My answer to her at the time was, 'There's no need to have a Plan B when God is in charge.' That would be my answer today, as well."*

CHAPTER 26

Before we knew it, Christmas was approaching. Nothing is as wonderful as Christmas with a baby in the house! There's the obvious connection to the Christ child that brings the true meaning of the season to life; in addition, the loving energy that flows from an infant seems to amplify the joy of the already glorious holiday. Emma was much too young to understand Christmas, although she was fascinated by the bright lights and soothed by the carols that often played in the background. Those of us who loved her, however, found that Emma's presence made the holiday season even more special.

As she grew more aware of her surroundings and the people in her life, Emma's visits with David seemed to evolve. She was now cooing and laughing, and the interaction between the two of them made David very happy. He saw her change with each visit, and I could see that he was amazed. In the weeks before Christmas, David brought Emma some very sweet gifts; his gestures touched my heart. I could see that for him, *she* was the best gift he had ever received. These were precious moments for him.

Ben and Rachel were feeling especially homesick during the holiday season, as you can imagine. This was not how they had envisioned their first Christmas with Emma. We knew they were yearning to be with their extended family and celebrate the holiday with them. When they asked Camille for permission to take Emma home for a short holiday visit, she immediately said yes. However, we needed to get David's permission, as well. This would present a new challenge; since the custody hearings began, we had put all mention of Ben and Rachel on hold. David was not aware that they were involved in any way.

I had become the main contact person with David over recent months because I saw him regularly. He and I had developed a comfortable relationship built on mutual respect. Sometimes I felt that being in the middle of such a fragile situation put me in an awkward position. Yet there was never a time when it caused difficulty, and I thank God for that. I prayed regularly for his help in handling things properly, and I always felt his presence.

During the next visit with David, I gently approached the subject of Ben and Rachel. I told David they were still part of Emma's life, just as he and Camille were. "This is important to Emma because of the bonding that took place in her early weeks of life," I explained. David seemed to understand. I then cautiously asked him if he would allow them to take Emma home to be with their family for Christmas. Looking back, I realize this was a lot to ask because it meant that Emma would be with others over the holiday, and he would not see her. I truly doubted that David would be in favor of this scenario, and I was surprised when he agreed to the request. Together we worked out a revised visitation schedule that made up for the time Emma would be gone. I sincerely appreciated his thoughtfulness toward Ben and Rachel. My respect for David grew more and more.

So Emma spent her first Christmas far away with Ben and Rachel and their family. We were honestly very happy for all of them, yet the house felt so empty when she was gone. We missed her terribly. As difficult as it was, however, I knew this was a good opportunity for us to experience life as it would be when the adoption took place. After all, this was what we were working toward—for Emma's sake.

Ben and Rachel returned after Christmas and reported that it had been wonderful to be with their family again. The visit had lifted their spirits, and I was so thankful for that. They told us that everyone was thrilled to have Emma in their midst again, as it had been months since they had seen her. There had been many hugs and kisses in those few days. There had also been many questions and concerns about the adoption placed before Ben and Rachel, who had no answers to share.

As the final days of the year drew to a close, our two families were looking forward to spending a quiet New Year's Eve together at home. We were hopeful that the new year was going to bring a positive resolution to the situation with Emma's adoption. We were going to toast to that.

David had a scheduled visitation early in the evening on New Year's Eve. As I waited for him to arrive, I wondered what God had planned for the year ahead. I waited, and wondered, for a very long time. I didn't hear from David. For the first time since the visitations began, he did not come to see Emma.

SOME MAY ASK ...

> *"Did you try to contact David?"*

TO YOU I SAY ...

> *"No. I trusted that I would hear from him when he was ready. In the meantime, I wondered how significant his absence was going to be in the big picture. Were his visits with Emma losing their importance to him?"*

CHAPTER 27

David called the following afternoon, New Year's Day, and apologized for missing his visit with Emma. He simply said something had come up, and he wasn't able to make it. I told him I understood that things can happen unexpectedly, and I encouraged him to call when he was unable to come to see Emma as scheduled. We agreed that he would just pick up where he left off and continue with the scheduled visits.

On one hand, I was a little concerned. It wasn't like David to take the visitation lightly. He had never even been late for a visit, much less not shown up. On the other hand, I remembered what Phillip had told Camille and me: birth fathers often lose interest after a while. I was reluctant to jump to that conclusion after only one missed visit, but I must be honest and say that it ignited a small flicker of hope in my heart. It ignited a *flame* of hope in the hearts of Ben and Rachel, who desperately clung to anything that might mean this ordeal was coming to a close.

~ 🦋 ~

As January turned into February, our household settled back into life as it had been before the holidays. Emma was growing bigger each day, and a very sweet personality was developing. Ours was a happy home; each of us loved returning to Emma and her parents at the end of the day. Sadie had a cute little song she sang to Emma when she came home, and it was music to my ears. Camille had special time with Emma, as well. When she walked in the door after work each day, she immediately reached out to hold the little one. Paul loved talking animatedly to Emma in the evenings; we all laughed at her reaction to his silliness. As for me, I found simple joy in rocking her as she fell asleep in my arms.

Ben and Rachel, who remained grateful to be with Emma all these months, continued to be torn. Joy? Yes, there was joy. They were the parents of a precious child who fulfilled their every dream. Yet they were still doing the juggling act of balancing their lives, old and new, and finding it more and more challenging each day. Growing discouraged at times, they were strengthened by their faith and their deep love for Emma. I did my best to encourage and support them, now more than ever. I also did my best to give encouragement and support to Camille, who was also growing impatient. At this moment in time, it was difficult for each of them to see the light at the end of the tunnel. For me, the light at the end of the tunnel was God, and I strongly sensed his presence.

Another court hearing had passed, bringing even more stress to everyone involved. At the beginning of the hearing, everything seemed to be the same. Camille was to retain temporary custody of Emma, and David's visitations were to continue, as scheduled. Following that declaration, however, the judge ordered Camille and David to attend parenting classes and a mediation class, as well. Phillip explained that the next step would be for the judge to assign a social worker to assess Emma's situation. This would include an evaluation of both Camille and David. While we were all getting a bit weary of the ongoing process, it seemed as if there was finally some momentum.

During moments of discouragement, Camille questioned why it was necessary to have to go through all of these steps. Actually, she knew the answer; it was the required procedure for the situation. Although in *our* minds we envisioned Emma going home with Ben and Rachel permanently, that is not what was before the court. We had to walk each step of the way, as it was presented to us. And we needed to continue to be strong.

On the day of the recent hearing, Camille, Phillip, and I were sitting on a bench outside the courtroom, waiting for our turn to see the judge. Camille was talking to Phillip, who was offering her guidance and support. After he explained what would take place during the hearing, Phillip asked how little Emma was doing. Camille told him Emma was doing very well. She explained that the prospective adoptive parents were in place as her parents because we believed that everything was going to work out, as planned. Phillip looked at Camille and said, "Emma *is* living with you, isn't she?" Matter-of-factly, Camille replied, "They all are." I still smile when I remember the look on Phillip's face. He shook his head from side to side and said with a grin, "This is the craziest case I've ever had!"

SOME MAY ASK ...

> *"Did you ever worry that Phillip would disapprove of Emma's current living arrangement?"*

TO YOU I SAY ...

> *"Early on, I had shared with Phillip my belief that God had chosen Ben and Rachel to be Emma's parents. He understood that our main concern, at this point, was to do what was best for Emma. A man of faith, Phillip was willing to honor our choices, which were within the framework of the law."*

CHAPTER 28

David continued with the visitations each week. Following the latest court hearing, however, I noticed that he seemed to be more distant and less engaged. While he obviously still adored his little girl, he was clearly discouraged like the rest of us. He hadn't expected the process to take so long or to be so involved, and he was growing restless with the structured visitation plan. I understood. Even though he clearly enjoyed his time with Emma, it was probably a bit boring to spend those two hours, three times a week, in the living room of our home. At the hearing, David's attorney had requested that he be allowed to take Emma outside our home for the visitations. For reasons unknown to me, the judge denied this request until the evaluations had been completed.

In the bleak winter weeks that followed, one very important change emerged. The formerly consistent pattern of visitations became more sporadic. David was not always on time, as he had been earlier, and he often changed visitation times to accommodate his schedule. I was able to be flexible, so the time changes weren't a problem. What I noticed, however, was a shift in David's demeanor. Where he used to be warm and friendly, he was now less interested in chatting before his time with Emma. During the visits, he was often on his cell phone, talking or listening to music.

I often wondered what was responsible for the changes in the visits that had previously brought such joy to David—and to me, as I watched him with Emma. Was the judge's refusal to allow him to take Emma out for visitations at the root of the change? Was he growing tired of jumping through all the legal hoops to gain custody of his little girl? Was he disappointed that, despite coming to Camille's home all these months, no relationship had developed between them? I realized the change in attitude could have been attributed to any one of these reasons, or all of them.

Doing my best to be sensitive to whatever David was experiencing, I tried to talk with him about how he was feeling. Without being intrusive, I wanted to understand what was going on in his mind. I told him I knew it was discouraging that this process seemed to go on forever. Unsure if he was traveling this road alone, I asked if he had support from close friends or family members. He was welcome, I told him, to bring any of them with him to our home for visitation. Rather than sit in judgment, I wanted to give David every benefit of the doubt.

Although I had faith that David would not be given custody of Emma at the end of this journey, I cared about him as a person. I knew God cared about him, too. As I said earlier, when I saw the feelings David had for his child, I learned a great lesson about the power of love. I realized it wasn't just the end result—Emma's adoption—I needed to pray about. My prayers also needed to be about the journey along the way, that we would walk the road with dignity and grace and kindness toward each other. My prayers needed to include each and every one of us who were on this journey. At this point, David was foremost in my prayers.

I was hoping my conversation with David would bring positive changes in the visitations, but things remained the same. There were more sporadic requests to reschedule, as well as late starts and shorter visits. David often appeared preoccupied, and it seemed to me the visits were no longer a priority for him. Having said this, however, it was clear that whenever David was with Emma, his love for her never wavered. Of that I was certain.

It was soon after our conversation that I discovered the reason for the change I had seen in David and the visitations. I guess I should have seen it coming. Sadie shared with me that she had read online, in David's own words, that he had a new girlfriend. He wrote in his profile that he was happy to have this new relationship in his life. The young woman meant a great deal to him, he wrote, and he adored her young daughter, as well. This explained everything.

SOME MAY ASK ...

> *"How did you react to the news of David's new
> girlfriend?"*

TO YOU I SAY ...

> *"I smiled. It instantly became clear to me that,
> nothing short of miraculous, this could be the
> answer to many prayers.'"*

CHAPTER 29

With April came Easter—and hope. I have always delighted in this special holiday, with its focus on new life and the fulfillment of God's promises. And I love the gift of spring that accompanies it. This year, Easter brought extra joy to our household. News of David's new girlfriend gave us hope that he was moving on with his life. We told ourselves that perhaps this would shift his focus from his fight for Emma to new beginnings.

In the entryway of our home hangs a beautiful wooden butterfly with a cross carved in the middle. It has great significance to me, at Easter and always, because my mother gave it to our family when the girls were young. A very spiritual woman, Mom hoped it would remind us of God's great love for us and his promise to always be with us. Years later, it's also a reminder to me that Mom is always with us. At the end of her life on earth, Mom asked me to tell her grandchildren to remember her whenever they see a butterfly. That simple request is an ongoing gift that we treasure—in nature and in our home.

One beautiful day during that month of April, I saw a butterfly flying outside my window, and I thought of Mom. Silently, I began to tell her how much I missed her, and soon I found myself pouring out my heart to her about Emma. There's no doubt in my mind that Mom is aware of everything that is taking place in the family she dearly loves, and I believe she continues to watch over us from heaven. On that day, I asked her to watch over *all* of us—our two families and David—in the weeks ahead.

On the wings of hope, Ben and Rachel took Emma to spend Easter with their family. Another three months had passed since their loved ones had last seen Emma, and they were overjoyed to be with their sweet baby again. They delighted in the changes they saw; they couldn't believe how much she had grown! Adding to their joy was the possibility that an end to their separation was in sight, and they might soon be together as a family. We shared their hope.

In the midst of the excitement, however, I forced myself to calm down. Perhaps we were premature in our joy; perhaps we were getting ahead of ourselves and the situation. After all, we were basing our hope on something unknown. No one had spoken to David to ask about his new relationship or his intentions. It seemed too soon to do that. After I thought about it at length, I secretly questioned whether this shift in circumstances would cause David to give up his fight for Emma. I told myself we needed to take one day at a time and be wise about this.

Actually, I knew it was God who was telling me. Holding my breath, I took his advice.

The month of April was significant for another reason. It had been nine months since Emma's birth. For some reason, Paul had believed the process of Emma's adoption—if there was to be an adoption—would take nine months. He had told Rachel, "Camille carried Emma for nine months of her pregnancy. Think of this time of waiting for the adoption as *your* pregnancy with Emma." Of course, as we began to walk the path of this journey, none of us wanted to believe it could conceivably take that long. Now, as we entered the ninth month, I prayed that Paul had been correct.

At this point, the plan was for me to talk with David sometime in the future about the positive changes in his life, to tell him I understood he had met someone special. Eventually, I would bring up the topic of the adoption once again. I trusted that God would let me know when it was the right time for this conversation to take place. I was perfectly content to wait for his nudge. I was feeling a great deal of pressure, however, from Ben, Rachel, and Camille, who wanted to move forward right away. I understood they were eager to find resolution after all these months. I was eager, too, but I knew it would be a mistake to approach David before the time was right. It felt a bit like push was coming to shove, but I held my ground and waited to hear from God.

SOME MAY ASK …

> *"Since there was not agreement regarding the appropriate time to talk to David, did this create a conflict in your relationships with Ben, Rachel, and Camille?"*

TO YOU I SAY …

> *"Not permanently, although there was some tension in the household for a while. It was nothing like the tension that would follow, however."*

CHAPTER 30

Although it's difficult to describe, other than to say it's an intuitive awareness, I soon felt the nudge from God. I knew the time was right for me to sit down and talk with David. I was a bit nervous, to say the least. There was a period when the visitations first began that David and I found it easy to talk; a trust was developing between us, and we were comfortable with each other. However, over recent weeks— perhaps since the new year began—the visits felt a little strained. David didn't seem to be himself.

As he was leaving our home after one of his visits, I asked David if we could talk the next time he came to see Emma. He seemed a little taken aback, and I wondered what was going through his mind. "There's nothing to worry about," I assured him. "I just want to chat." Watching him walk to his car that day, I prayed for God's blessings. I asked him to ease David's concern and open his mind to what I needed to say, and I asked him to give me the wisdom and strength to handle our conversation well.

Many months had led up to this. I knew it was going to be a very important step.

When David returned for the next visit, I greeted him at the door. We exchanged our usual small talk, and I handed Emma to him as we sat down. We played with her a bit to ease the tension, and then I began. I asked David how he was doing, and he replied that he was doing well. He went on to say that he had someone special in his life. David seemed happy when he talked about his girlfriend; it was clear he cared about her very much. He was glad to be in this relationship, he told me, but his life had become complicated with all the pieces that needed his attention. I could only imagine.

After we had talked for a while, I gently brought up the issue of the adoption. I felt as if I was walking on eggshells as I began to address the subject. I made it clear that I could see how much David adored Emma. I told him I had developed a great deal of respect for him during the months of visitations. I knew he wanted the best for Emma, and I knew he wanted what was best for him, as well. I asked him what that looked like to him at this time. Was he still focused on raising Emma himself, or was he willing to consider other options as a possible "best" for all involved?

David really didn't take much time before he said he still intended to raise Emma. I nodded in understanding, and then I asked how that would work out if his relationship continued to become more serious. Had he considered that it would be difficult to raise a baby on his own, in addition to working to support her *and* also nurturing an evolving adult relationship? Did he have any idea how much it cost to raise a child—in time and energy and money?

I assured David that I wasn't looking for an answer from him at this moment in time. I was just pointing out some things for him to consider. I reiterated that I sincerely cared about him as a person, and I wanted him to understand all the options available to him. Because David had consistently resisted the idea of Emma's adoption, we had never had much discussion about open adoption. Open adoption would allow both birth parents to have a connection with Emma as she grew up, according to a plan agreed upon by all parties. I gave David some written information about this and told him that Ben and Rachel were willing to discuss it with him and Camille.

This, of course, opened a new door. It was time to tell David that Ben and Rachel had been living at our house with Emma all these months. I anticipated that he might be angry or feel deceived, but when I told him our reasons for this—all of them centered on Emma's well-being—he seemed to accept the situation without question. While David had initially clung to the idea of raising Emma, I sensed he was now willing to listen to what was being presented to him. That was all I was asking of him.

SOME MAY ASK …

> "Were you hoping you could convince David during
> this conversation to change his mind about raising
> Emma?"

TO YOU I SAY …

> "Not at all. That was not my intention, and I
> knew it wasn't part of God's plan at this point,
> either. I truly felt that I was guided to place the
> considerations before David, as honestly as I
> could, and encourage him to take time for serious
> thought."

Chapter 31

My conversation with David continued. Like Camille, he was required to follow through with the judge's requests from the previous court hearing. This meant that he had classes to attend and child support to pay; in addition, attorney's fees were piling up. I knew David did not have the financial help that Camille did. Added to the other complications in his life, I suspected all of this was burdensome. As we talked, I wanted David to know that allowing Emma to be adopted by caring parents was not about weakness on his part; it was about strength and it was about love. I knew he loved her very much, and I knew she loved him, as well.

Was it an easy conversation? Definitely not. Throughout the discussion with David, I wanted to be as sensitive as possible. This was of utmost importance to me. I wanted him to be treated with the respect that he deserved. This was an extremely significant event in his life, a very emotional period. The best I could hope for—pray for—was that the end result would bring him a sense of peace. David, like

Camille, was not faith-driven, but I knew this didn't matter. God would be looking out for him, just as he was looking out for us. That is how God operates.

Finally, I had to take our discussion to a place I dreaded going. It was a harsh truth, but it had to be addressed. I told David there was one other thing he needed to consider as part of the equation. As gently as I could, I explained to him what Phillip had earlier explained to us: if David and Camille each continued to pursue custody of Emma, Camille—as mother—would almost assuredly be awarded primary custody. I added that Camille was determined to continue the fight for custody, although I secretly wondered to myself how that scenario would play out.

"Camille's attorney has advised us that this is the way the court seems to lean," I told David. If both parents are deemed equally qualified, for lack of a better word, the court decision usually favors the mother. This meant that David would possibly be looking at a future of visitations and child support, rather than living out his dream of raising Emma. I told David I knew this didn't seem fair, but we had been told that it was the reality of the situation.

The sad thing is that I don't think David's attorney had been very thorough in his approach to the case. He often seemed unprepared in court, and he didn't appear to be very professional. I didn't get the impression that he had covered all the bases with David, preparing him for the various steps and explaining all possible outcomes. Phillip, our attorney, had been very clear with Camille and me along the way. While we didn't always like what we heard, we were thankful he was honest and forthcoming with us. I felt bad that David had not received the same consideration. I encouraged him to talk to his attorney and ask the important questions, rather than take my word for it.

Our conversation that day was long and difficult, but I thought it had gone reasonably well. David and I had both shared from our hearts and presented things as we saw them. I understood completely where David was coming from. He wanted Emma in his life. I couldn't blame him for that. To be honest, I wanted her in my life, too. Once again, I asked David to consider open adoption, which would allow him to continue to have Emma in his life without the heavy responsibility of raising her. I hoped he would think about what was best for Emma.

When he left that evening, I had no idea what was going through David's mind. I didn't need to know. What was important to me was that I had done what I had been asked to do; God would do the rest. This story was going to unfold exactly as it was meant to, and we would deal with whatever lay ahead. That was not exactly the message that Camille, Ben, and Rachel wanted to hear, but it was the only message I could offer. We needed to trust in God's wisdom from here on out. Emma's future was in his hands.

SOME MAY ASK ...

> *"How were you able to simply place Emma's future in God's hands after all you had invested in the situation?"*

TO YOU I SAY ...

> *"There were many elements involved. The strongest reason behind my 'surrender' was my faith that God would make everything right, according to his will. This was foremost in my mind. Being human, however, my weakness also played a role. It had been an emotionally exhausting nine months, and I was relieved to relinquish Emma to God, knowing I had done all I could do."*

CHAPTER 32

These were uneasy days for each of us. All we could do was wait and pray. Ben and Rachel were extremely anxious about the outcome of my conversation with David. They were as emotionally exhausted as Camille and I were—even more so. They had so much going on in their lives. They had obligations to meet and responsibilities to uphold. Most importantly, they had a future to embark upon—hopefully with Emma. It had been a long, difficult journey for them.

Camille was on edge, too. She felt the anxiety of Ben and Rachel, which translated into pressure on her. The waiting, and not being able to do anything more, was creating an underlying tension. I prayed that Emma was not sensing it, although I suspected that on some level she was. I did my best to focus on the positive and to nurture a sense of peace in the home. After all these months, I was desperate for things to turn out well for everyone. I was desperate for God to make things right.

In the meantime, we waited to hear if David had changed his mind. He came for visit after visit with Emma, but he never brought up the subject of adoption. Without asking him directly, I tried to get an intuitive sense of what he was feeling, to no avail. It didn't seem right to push him; I knew he had a lot to think about. Really, the ball was now in David's court, and I felt we needed to give him time and space to think the situation through.

One afternoon, as the weather began to show signs of spring, I went outside to tend to my roses. I needed some time alone, and nothing makes me happier than to work in my gardens. It was a perfect opportunity to talk with God, to let him know what was in my heart. "God," I told him, "you know I trust in you completely. I believe this situation with Emma will have a happy ending, and I believe you're at work in all our lives. I want to say that I will honor your timing, God, but the reality is that I'm faltering here. This is taking its toll on our two families and David, too. Please, *please*, can there be some resolution soon?"

During my silent conversation with God, Rachel came out to the garden. I knew she was having an especially rough day, consumed with worry about what the future would bring. I had tried to lift her spirits earlier that morning, but I had met with little success. Standing beside me with tears in her eyes, Rachel urged me to confront David *now* about his decision. "This has gone on too long," she cried. "He *has* to let us have Emma." At that emotionally raw moment,

I wanted so badly to be able to say the words that would bring Rachel comfort. Instead, I could only be realistic and say, "Rachel, I wish I could say what you want to hear, but the reality is that David doesn't have to relinquish Emma. It's not our decision to make. We can only have faith that God will act soon." For me, the message was anchored in hope, but I knew the words seemed weak and shallow to Rachel. This was one of the most difficult moments of our journey.

It was at this very time, when each of us seemed to be at the end of our rope, that things began to change swiftly. Isn't that how it often is? Just when, despite the depth of your faith, you think you can't take one more day of tension, pain, or uncertainty, you find that your prayers have been answered. And they are often answered in ways much more wonderful than you could have possibly imagined. That is how it was for us.

All of a sudden, as the month of May began to unfold, David missed a number of visits in a row. There were excuses at first and then no word from him at all. It was as if he had simply walked out of the picture. How could this be, after all these months? We were contemplating what our next step should be when Camille received a phone call from Christine. She had exciting news to share with us: David was willing to talk about adoption.

SOME MAY ASK ...

"How did all of you respond to this news?"

TO YOU I SAY ...

"We were on cloud nine! I had a distinct sense
that we were finally nearing the end of our ordeal,
and I no longer felt the need to express caution or
advise the others to refrain from getting their hopes
up. My hopes were up! Previously united by our
devotion to Emma, we were now united in joy.
This had been a long time coming!"

CHAPTER 33

As I write this part of my story, I struggle with how to paint the picture of our happy ending. Let me begin with Ben and Rachel. With the shift in circumstances surrounding Emma, Ben and Rachel began to focus on working out an agreement for an open adoption with David, as well as Camille. They sincerely wanted it to be an agreement that was acceptable to all. This was done through mediation with Christine, who had now taken over from Phillip. After the revelation that David was willing to allow Ben and Rachel to adopt Emma, Phillip's work was done. He had served Camille and Emma well, and we will be eternally grateful to him.

It was truly a blessing to me to see the happiness and joy that Ben and Rachel now felt. Gone were the fear and the palpable anxiety that had hung over them in recent months. Their thoughts now turned to the bright future that lay ahead for the three of them—father, mother, and child. It was as if a huge weight had been lifted; indeed it had. Family and friends back home began to look forward to their return. Finally, life was going to settle into a place of contentment for this young family. We were very happy for them.

Christine told Camille that David's decision to proceed with the adoption had come from his desire to move on with his life. After speaking with his attorney, he accepted the apparent futility of his dream of gaining full custody of Emma. A lifetime of visitations, even visitations with more privileges, was not what he was looking for. Years of child support payments seemed overwhelming.

Despite all we had been through to reach this conclusion, I felt sad for David. My heart still hurts for him today. I was thankful, however, that God's plan included the opportunity for David to have new joy in his life, with his girlfriend and her little girl. While I knew neither of them could ever take the place of Emma, they offered new paths to happiness. I prayed that everything would work out exactly as David wanted.

Just as Ben and Rachel felt tremendous relief with David's decision, Camille was able to shed her own blanket of anxiety. Knowing she had done the best she could for her little angel, she would be able to completely move ahead with her life. Camille was relieved that her daughter was forever going to be with parents who adored her and would give her everything she needed in life. "That's all I ever wanted, Mom," she softly told me. I was very proud of Camille at this moment, just as I was very proud of her every step along the way. Looking back, I am still very proud—more than words can ever say.

Paul and I were swallowed up in everyone's feelings of joy and relief. Personally, we shared a sense of completion. I want to say it felt like a job well done, but that sounds trite. It was not a job; it was a journey, and I was thankful we had walked it together. I knew Paul was eager to get on with our life, just as Camille, Ben, and Rachel were eager to get on with theirs. It had been a long time since life seemed normal, if there is such a thing. First came the cancer diagnosis and the chemotherapy treatment, and then little Emma had arrived. We wondered where life's path would take us now. *Hopefully to a place of serenity,* I thought.

The battle for Emma, if it can be called a battle, was over. In the big picture, everyone had won. Who could ask for more? First and foremost, I was overwhelmed with thankfulness to God for his ongoing goodness. He had been present through all the hard times—supporting us and guiding us. I was aware that his goodness was extended to David, as well. Of course it would be. That's what I love about my God.

Mother's Day was fast approaching, and I marveled at the thought of Rachel spending her first Mother's Day in her own home with her precious child. What a beautiful scenario! No one but God could have planned it that way. As soon as the legal paperwork was in place, our little Emma would be returning to her life far away. I was trying hard to focus on the joy and the thankfulness, but inside my heart was aching. The reality of loss, which I had refused to face all these months, could no longer be ignored.

SOME MAY ASK ...

> *"What were your last days with Emma and her
> parents like?"*

TO YOU I SAY ...

> *"Ben, who had come to spend a few last days with our
> family, returned to their home to prepare for Emma's
> arrival. We said our happy/sad goodbyes to him as
> he left for their new adventure as a family. Rachel
> stayed behind with Emma to complete the final steps
> of the adoption. I treasured every moment we had
> with Emma and her mommy, painfully aware that
> these wonderful days were coming to an end."*

CHAPTER 34

As the day approached for Emma and Rachel to leave, our family and friends expressed the need to say goodbye. These people were a loving network of support we had relied on for strength along the way. They had grown to love this little girl and her parents, and they were going to miss them, too. With that in mind, we planned a little get-together. Rather than a farewell party, it was to be a celebration of love and joy.

Our house was filled with laughter and happiness on that beautiful spring evening. As each person arrived, I thought of his or her place in our story. Whether it was a card sent on a tough day, a phone call of encouragement, the willingness to listen to frustration and fears, or the always-welcome prayers on Emma's behalf, these special people had done God's work on earth. I was—and forever will be—abundantly grateful to each and every one of them.

As everyone marveled at the good news of her adoption, Emma was lovingly passed from lap to lap. She received hugs and kisses from all. In the midst of the excitement,

Rachel made a point to thank her new friends and family for their support. "It's meant so much to Ben and me," she told them. I remember looking at Rachel as she spoke and thinking how generous she was to let us have this one last moment with Emma, her daughter. I will never forget how that touched my heart.

Much too quickly, the gathering came to an end and people began to leave. Our immediate family was left to say our goodbyes to Rachel and Emma, who would soon be on their way to join Ben at their home. Although our hearts were heavy, we reminded ourselves that this wasn't actually goodbye; it was simply a new beginning. With Christine's help, Camille, Ben, and Rachel had drawn up an open adoption agreement that would allow us to be part of Emma's and her parents' lives forever. Still, it was a bittersweet moment. We had been together more than nine months, and we were going to miss them terribly.

And so the hugs began. First Rebecca said her tender goodbyes to Rachel and Emma. Rebecca, who loves children and walks her faith daily, had been a ray of sunshine to all of us whenever she visited. We were thankful for the light she brought during the tough times. Sadie was next to give Emma a hug. Sadie was especially sad; she had grown very close to little Emma over these past months, and she dreaded seeing her leave. Paul, doing his best to remain strong during his goodbyes, fought back tears as he hugged Emma and her mommy. Rachel, like Ben, had become both a friend and a part of our family, and we loved them very much.

Camille reached for Emma after Paul gave his final hug. This was what she had worked so hard for all these months, to make certain that Emma would have what she deserved in life. Yet I could see the pain from the past return to Camille's eyes as she held Emma close. She tried to hide her strong emotions as she told her little angel to be a good girl for her mommy and daddy. The moment took my breath away. It was so difficult to watch Camille's heart break once again. I said a silent prayer that God would help that tender heart heal, as only he can.

Finally, it was my turn. I gave Rachel a big hug and told her how much she and her family meant to us. She graciously thanked me for all we had done to bring Emma into their lives. With a smile on my face, I told her God was responsible for this miracle. I repeated what I had said many times before: God was with all of us these past months, and he would be with each of us in the future as we continued on our paths in life. We must never forget that.

As I reached for little Emma, my precious granddaughter, I was filled with an abundance of different emotions—joy, awe, and sadness, to name a few. Emma's life up to this point was so short, yet we had traveled the journey of a lifetime to get there. That night she was as soft and cuddly as ever. As I held her, she drew close and rested her little cheek next to mine in a way she had never done before. It was a little piece of heaven on earth. "God," I prayed silently, "I love this little girl so much! Thank you for bringing her into my life."

Handing Emma back to Rachel was almost more painful than I could bear. It was not nearly as difficult, however, as watching them drive away from our home.

SOME MAY ASK ...

"What are things like today?"

TO YOU I SAY ...

"The miracle continues ..."

CHAPTER 35

Some may ask ... "And what about today? How do your lives intertwine in the here and now?" I am extremely grateful to be able to say that the blessings of the past continue to bless us in the present. Ever-so-thankful, I praise God for the gift of Emma in our lives! His magnificent choreography continues to amaze us and bring us joy. Emma is growing into a beautiful young girl, who warms our hearts and makes us smile. She is an integral part of our family, and we are privileged to have a place in her family, as well.

Each month, our family receives a delightful e-mail. Every letter is written from Emma's perspective by her sweet, and very talented, mommy. In childlike words and wonder, we are able to hear what is going on in her life. We get such joy from these e-mails and the pictures that accompany them. When one of the family discovers the e-mail, we excitedly text or call the others to announce that "Emma-mail" has arrived. It's one of the highlights of my life to read those letters and look at those pictures!

In addition to the treasured e-mails, we have wonderful weekend visits from Emma and her family, and we travel to visit them, as well. It is such fun to be together, to see how Emma has grown and to reminisce—with laughter and a few tender tears—about the journey that brought us all to this point.

I often sit back and watch Camille with Emma during their visits, and I see something beautiful between the two—something difficult to explain. While one day, at her parents' discretion, Emma will learn that Camille is her birth mother, for now Camille is simply a member of the extended family who loves her very much. As I watch the two of them together, my heart overflows. I treasure their little tea parties and bubble-blowing sessions; I love watching Camille show Emma how she crochets. And I have to admit that it makes me chuckle to see Camille's independent spirit in the child she brought to life. All of this is the icing on the cake—abundant blessings for our family.

Today Emma has a new little adopted brother who is also adored by one and all—especially his big sister! Young Mark's arrival into this special family is another amazing story of God's work in our lives. It serves to remind us, yet again, that he is in charge and miracles happen when we are open to his power and goodness.

Camille continues on the positive path she began before Emma was born. All these years later, she still works at the promising job she held during the pregnancy. Following

Emma's birth, she met Seth, a nice young man who helped fill the painfully empty spot that was left in her heart. A coincidence? Absolutely not. At the time, it was clear to me that God was responsible for knowing exactly what Camille needed and bringing it into her life.

Camille and Seth have been together for many years. From the beginning of their relationship, Seth was aware of the situation with Emma, and he has respected that part of Camille's life. He supports her in her efforts to stay connected to Emma. For her part, Camille has found a way to balance Emma's place in her life with a healthy separation. She is thankful her little angel remains in her life, but she respects that Emma has her own family—a wonderful family. Camille seems to have found her peace with a situation that could have been the source of lifelong pain. More prayers answered …

I know that some may ask about David—where he fits into Emma's life at the present time. Because I don't want this to be the final focus of my story, I'll address it now in the best way I can. We have not kept in touch with David; we don't know where he is or what he's doing with his life. In this age of technology, I suppose we could find the answers to those questions, but we have chosen not to do that. While the open adoption agreement allows him to keep in touch with Emma through her parents, I am aware that he has made little effort to do so. Although we are not connected, I continue to keep David in my prayers. I know that Rachel prays for him, as well.

I realize that not all open adoptions have a happy ending like this one, although I wish it could be so. I also recognize that this open arrangement has been successful because of the faithfulness of Emma's adoptive parents. Without them, this chapter could not have been written. In the very beginning of Emma's journey, Camille, Paul, and I made a commitment to Ben and Rachel to fight for Emma's adoption because we believed God had chosen them to be Emma's parents. We were faithful to our promise. Later, they made an equally significant promise to us to include us in Emma's life, and they have been faithful to their promise. This is what cooperation and appreciation and, most significantly, the love of Christ look like to me.

I don't need to repeat that Emma is a source of ongoing joy for our family, but I will. Life has taken on new meaning since she arrived. The greatest joy, however, comes from knowing that God, in his infinite wisdom, has worked wonders through the birth of this child. I am so thankful. I am thankful Camille chose to carry her child. I am thankful for the support she received during and following Emma's birth. I am thankful the prayers of two loving parents were answered with adoption of this beautiful little girl. I am thankful we all had the strength and perseverance to follow the path that God laid out for us.

That is the bottom line. I am thankful for God's great choreography, the ribbon that ties everything together. And while I know that anything is possible with God, I will forever call our story of Emma what I believe it to be—a miracle of love.